PRAISE FOR *PERFECTLY UNFINISHED*

Transparent, heartfelt, encouraging—here's the dramatic, true story of Andrea Logan White's journey from the Playboy Mansion to Jesus. You'll be inspired and challenged by what she learned on her path toward redemption and hope.

Lee Strobel, *New York Times* bestselling author of *The Case for Christ* and *The Case for Faith*

Nothing fills the hungry heart like infinite love and acceptance. And with every chapter of *Perfectly Unfinished*, we are assured again and again that we are not alone and that the Spirit of God speaks to us, perhaps most of all and best of all through God's people who have been most broken. Thank you, Andrea Logan White, for learning to love yourself, because in this discovery, so many of your "sisters" will learn to do the same.

Robin Givens, actress, author, and mom

Perfectly Unfinished is raw, real, and inspiring. With courage, strength, and vulnerability, Andrea Logan White shares the struggles she endured and the freedom she discovered as a woman, wife, and mother when she learned to fully surrender her life to the Lord. Starting every chapter with inspiring Scripture, Andrea reminds us that even in our weakest and most desperate times, God's love is still readily available, and he is longing for us to accept it. This book is encouraging and LIFEsaving.

Alexa Vega, actress

PERFECTLY UNFINISHED

PERFECTLY UNFINISHED

FINDING BEAUTY IN THE MIDST OF BROKENNESS

Andrea Logan White

with Cindy Lambert

ZONDERVAN

Perfectly Unfinished
Copyright © 2017 by Andrea Logan White

Requests for information should be addressed to:
Zondervan, *3900 Sparks Dr. SE, Grand Rapids, Michigan 49546*

ISBN 978-0-310-34533-6 (softcover)

ISBN 978-0-310-35051-4 (audio)

ISBN 978-0-310-34534-3 (ebook)

Disclaimer: The author has made her best effort to re-create events, locales, and conversations from memory. Some names and identifying details have been changed to protect the privacy of individuals.

Andrea Logan White is represented by The Litton Group, a brand management and content strategy agency in Brentwood, Tennessee. Learn more at www.TheLittonGroup.com.

Cover photo: Christine Comina McCrudden
Interior design: Kait Lamphere

First printing August 2017 / Printed in the United States of America

To my precious family,
and to all who long for perfection

CONTENTS

Chapter 1

THE VIEW FROM
THE RED CARPET

> And let us run with perseverance the race marked out
> for us, fixing our eyes on Jesus, the pioneer and perfecter
> of faith.
>
> HEBREWS 12:1–2

Thank God, I am not the woman I once was.

But oh, how I long to be already a woman who dances peacefully through life with grace and beauty. A woman who shines in every storm and fully trusts that God is at work for her good and for his glory.

In other words, I want to be perfect. (I mean, really, is that asking too much?)

I want to be perfectly finished and all wrapped up in a beautiful package so that I can just enjoy a pleasant story of the rest of my life. I know I'm not the only woman who feels this way! We may vary a good bit in how we describe the perfection to which we aspire, but I meet women on a regular basis who share my struggle of coming up short of the women we want to be.

My ideal is to have a perfect marriage with amicable disagreements that always resolve in perfect unity. I want nightly dinners around the table, where my children sit still for more than four minutes and eat every bite of wholesome food on their well-portioned plates. I want a perfectly organized home that everyone in the house helps to keep tidy. I want to exercise and meditate and drink green juice and of course go to church every Sunday, on time with peaceful precision. And dare I say it: I'd love to wear white linen that I never spill on, and even when I embrace my child with dirty hands and muddy clothes, the linen would never soil. And oh, if I'm dreaming that big, I may as well throw in a shelf full of Oscars alongside my *New York Times* bestsellers.

Yes, perfect and finished. That's the dream.

Like the cast and crew at the gala premiere of our movie, *Mom's Night Out.*

○ ✤ ○

Flashes of light flickered so rapidly that it seemed like I was facing a hundred strobe lights.

"Over here to the right," a voice called. I turned and smiled. So many cameras clicked and voices competed to be heard that there was no way to please so many photographers (professionals and fans) at once. All I could do was keep turning and smiling.

"Group shot," someone called, so I moved in closer to my fellow cast members as we reached our arms around one another like old college friends at homecoming. What a fun way to enjoy our reunion of cast and crew.

"On your left. That's it. Perfect." I tried not to blink too often as black spots now dominated my vision.

I was having a blast at the gala red carpet premiere of our major motion picture, *Mom's Night Out*, at Grauman's Chinese Theatre. So, too, were my effervescent costars—Patricia Heaton (*Everyone Loves Raymond*), Sarah Drew (*Grey's Anatomy*), and Abbie Cobb (*Suburgatory*). Trace Adkins, towering a head taller than the rest of the cast in his signature black cowboy hat, was grinning from ear to ear. Sean Astin, used to such events, thanks to his starring role in the *Lord of the Rings* films, remained as relaxed and down-to-earth as a next-door neighbor enjoying a block party. Each red-carpet premiere that I've attended, before and after this one, has its own character, but thanks to this film being a comedy, this premiere was overflowing with laughter.

We had reason to celebrate. This was a big deal. It's always rewarding to experience a movie from its development all the way to the finished product, but not every movie is given the opportunity for a Grauman's gala—a high spot in the world of entertainment—and I was honored to have played a part in a movie so well received. How perfect, too, that *Mom's Night Out*, a celebration of the humor of motherhood and marriage, was releasing on Mother's Day weekend in 2014.

Though the faces of the crowd before me were lost in the sea of flashing cameras, I knew that my mom, and my dad and his girlfriend, Carol, were there, along with my older brother Jason. I was sorry my younger brother Josh and his family couldn't make it from Arizona, but I knew they would have been there if they could've. My grandparents on Mom's side (Dad's folks had passed) had also come to share this celebration, but I'd have to wait until the photo op was over before I'd be able to scan the crowd to enjoy the smiles on their faces again. To have my family share this event with me, given our complicated and painful history, was a gift.

I heard David's laugh off to my right somewhere, and even though I couldn't see him through the flashing lights, I easily pictured my husband's broad smile. I never took for granted his unwavering support of me. Then I spotted him, joking around with the film's producer, Kevin Downes. David and Kevin had been like brothers for more than twenty years. They'd been through so much life together—the hard times and the good times—and had even been occasional business partners. It simply seemed too good to be true that we three could celebrate this success together.

Finally the photo shoot and red carpet interviews wrapped up, and it was time to move into the theatre to watch our premiere. We were invited to proceed down the red carpet toward the doors of Grauman's Chinese Theatre. Dressed in a blueish-purple Grecian-style dress, I felt the sheer layers flowing in the slight breeze as David extended his arm and we stepped onto the famous red carpet and glided toward the golden double doors framed by massive red pillars that swept up to the dramatic, oversized red pagoda roof. Hollywood's historic landmark movie theatre.

To be a part of this moment moved me deeply, not because it was all about the film or all about the cast. It moved me because it marked another milestone in the unfolding drama of what God had been doing in my life in Hollywood. I had moved to Los Angeles at twenty years old with nothing more than a dream in my heart to act, and in the years leading up to this moment, David and I had come so far and grown so much in our understanding of the mission God was entrusting to us. Just two months before, we'd celebrated the premiere of *God's Not Dead*, and tonight was another celebration of our calling to become an influence in our culture through the media. We knew this was one more step in expanding that influence—a night to celebrate what God was doing and express our thankfulness to him. Given all that had transpired in the journey that brought us here together, I was awestruck that God knew all along that this moment was coming.

"It would be fun if the kids were here with us," I whispered to David as we proceeded down the carpet.

"I know," he said, "but we did the right thing in leaving them home. We'll take them to see it when we can focus entirely on them. Here they would have been overwhelmed by the crowd of reporters and fans." I knew he was right. It was just that I loved appearing in a comedy that not only made moms laugh, but also let them feel comfortable to bring their entire families to see. I was eager to share the movie with my own three kiddos and hear their laughter as they saw it for the first time.

Now here's the part you must not miss. Alongside the red carpet were red velvet ropes lined with fans and reporters and more cameras. What did the star-struck fans see as we strolled the carpet? They saw celebrities. Not Angelina Jolie and Brad Pitt, mind you, but celebrities who seem so . . . well . . . perfectly packaged, as if their lives are just as perfect in everyday life as they seem to be when they appear on the red carpet. From the outside looking in, it often appears that celebrities have it all together. No problems or worries, just moments of delight that give the impression that they possess something special. They saw David, my beautiful husband, dressed to the nines in his exquisite tuxedo and beautifully shined shoes. They saw my professionally fitted gown tailored to complement my figure, enhancing the illusion that I was gliding effortlessly down the red carpet.

You get the idea. What those lining the ropes were seeing was an *illusion* of the actor Andrea Logan White, apparently stepping effortlessly from her ideal job into the limelight of accolades and success.

But it's smoke and mirrors.

It's the magic of the movies.

It's the view through the camera's lens.

It is not real.

Real is David and I feeling distracted and overwhelmed as we prepared to head to the premiere, trying to make sure our kids were safe and settled. Earlier that morning, as I sat at the nail salon (a rare treat for me these days), I got a call from our au pair, crying. She was out running errands with my daughters Ocean and Everson (four and one, at the time).

Real is her explanation between hysterical sobs: "I had a little car accident." Real is my heart jumping into my throat with fear for my children. Once she assured me they were fine, I realized with relief that the cause of her hysteria was her fear that I would be angry. It took some convincing to assure her I wasn't angry—just relieved that no one was hurt.

Real is feeling fidgety, anxious, and distracted, right there on the red carpet, wondering if my girls were having frightening memories of the accident and my wanting to rush home to them.

Real is the number of hours the cast spent that very day preparing for the night's event, using the combined talents of makeup artists and clothing designers.

Real is the crowded hair-and-makeup trailer on the *Mom's Night Out* set, and waiting our turn while gagging on powder and hairspray fumes, running our lines with one another at 3:00 a.m. as we prepared for our scenes to be shot.

Real was the twisted, painful path that took me through the filming (all taking place at night), while running between scenes to nurse my newborn, Everson, and tend to my little ones, Ethan and Ocean.

And real is the journey of the script of this movie that bore little resemblance to the initial concept—an idea begun four years ago. An idea that had lots of starts and stops and ups and downs and challenges and conflicts and ugly moments and beautiful ones—until finally all of those combined into the finished product we now celebrated.

NOT YET FINISHED

On this night, the movie was finished. As finished as it ever will be. The final cut was made. The final effects were added. The film was in the can. It was all it was ever going to be.

But inside, *I am not finished*. I am a work in progress, being transformed from a mixed-up young woman into the child of God made in his image and growing ever so slowly in the knowledge of his love and character.

No matter how much I may long for a red-carpet kind of life, such fantasies of the perfect life can never be reality. I, like all of us, am imperfect and unfinished. But knowing that presents us with an opportunity. For there is something richly comforting (when understood) about being *unfinished*. When we are unfinished, there is still time to be perfected! A movie, once it's in the can, is as good as it will ever be. But you and I are still in progress. We can have great hope, and in that hope, true freedom.

I look into my heart—the heart of a woman saved by God's grace at the age of twenty-two, washed clean by the blood of Jesus, pulled out of the pit of self-destruction and despair more times than I can count, dearly loved and forgiven and gifted with more blessings than I can name—but even so, I often don't like what I see. Regardless of the image of Andrea Logan White portrayed to those watching at a movie premiere or hearing me speak of my relationship with God in an interview, I fall short in my faith and in my confidence in God's love. I am dreadfully, desperately, deeply flawed. I frequently suffer from the illusion that if only I could take control of my life and circumstances, I could perfect myself and my world—but every effort to do so backfires.

I meet and listen to and read about other believers who speak "from victory" and see those who flash brilliant, confident smiles in the face of adversity, but no matter how much I pray, how much Scripture I study, how hard I try, I am wholly flawed in my responses to life, and the faith that is supposed to be growing in my spirit is, to my eyes, glaringly unfinished.

I wrestle with God and often feel condemned when I'm in the middle of one of life's storms and can't seem to find my way out. I feel like a kid who has been told, "Good luck, kid; have fun with this one," and start to beat myself up with guilt and condemnation. I put on a brave face and forced smile and pretend that life is good, when in reality I can't seem to find peace in the midst of turmoil. I can't seem to find the beauty when I'm feeling broken, lost, and abandoned. It is then, especially, that my quest for perfection rears its ugly head and blames, accuses, and screams at me as if I should know better and have it all figured out. It's as if I'm waiting for that one precious nugget of spiritual truth that will instantly eradicate my self-condemnation and my failures and instead infuse me with spiritual insight and strength.

So far, that has not been God's response.

No flashing neon signs from heaven with neat little answers. No single Bible verse that suddenly unlocks the secret that always seems just beyond my grasp. There is nothing but the simple inner knowledge that it is my job to press on.

Just press on.

So, press on is what I do.

I've decided to take my next bold step of pressing on in the form of this book. It won't be all rainbows and unicorns. This is not the G-rated story of a good Christian girl being transformed effortlessly, but the R-rated story of a girl with a very messy life, who doubts, wrestles, and has a hard time accepting her suffering, whether it's suffering that is totally beyond her control, suffering that results from wandering into areas God never intended her to go, or suffering while following him exactly where he has led her.

I start with the confession that I am deeply conflicted. No matter how successful I become, how spiritual I grow, how loved I am, I am still enslaved by a lie the enemy has been using against me my entire life: *I feel I need to be perfect in order to be accepted—by myself, by others, by God*. And because of how imperfect I am, whether in choices I make or in my responses to circumstances beyond my control, my fear that I am not accepted and not loved by God or others often keeps holding me in its grasp.

Sound familiar? Are you repeatedly disappointed in your responses to the circumstances you face, the flaws that won't go away, the patterns you can't seem to break, and the ways you fall short of who you want to be?

Then you share my conundrum: longing for peace, for beauty, in the midst of an incredibly imperfect and broken life.

And here is the good news: Though there are no magic answers for those of us who know this struggle, there is, thanks to Jesus Christ, a wondrous mystery at work within this messy reality of our lives. So, let us together learn to live with this wondrous mystery and love our way through it.

I am on a twofold mission in this book:

- I want us to discover how to *see ourselves as God sees us today*, beautifully broken daughters being perfected by the immeasurable love of our Savior.
- I want us to discover how to *be ourselves just as we are*, unfinished, yet resting in God's peace.

We may not be there yet, but according to the verse at the beginning of this chapter, we don't need to be. For it is God, not we, who has pioneered our faith, and it is God, not we, who will finish it. Our job is just to show up—just as I am, as you are—and open ourselves wide to all that God wants to accomplish in us and through us.

I'm ready to follow our pioneer and perfecter. Join me.

Chapter 2

THE SCRIPT

Jesus said, "It is finished." With that, he bowed his head
and gave up his spirit.

JOHN 19:30

Writing this book has not been anything like I pictured. Not even close.

In anticipation of writing, I'd had lots of fun romanticizing it. After all, David and I are movie makers. I had toyed with scenes of me at my desk, Bible open before me, light streaming through the window, wiping wistful tears from my cheeks while jotting inspiring words of what I've learned through the struggles of an imperfect and unfinished life. Flipping through old journals and photos would spark memories of key turning points. You can picture it, can't you? Add some soft-focus visual effects and a touching soundtrack. David enters stage right, kisses the top of my head, and then tiptoes across the softly lit hall to kiss our sleeping children tucked snugly in their beds. He glances back at me, poised gracefully at my desk, my long blonde hair falling softly along my neck.

Cut.

Okay. Absurd, right? And *way* over the top! I agree. So dump that scene on the cutting room floor among the clutter of doll clothes, colorful building blocks, and the TV remote that I almost tripped over on my way to the kitchen counter to get the child-strength acetaminophen. I push my unwashed hair from my eyes and look at the clock for the umpteenth time. Still many hours before David gets home this evening. Too bad. I'm in desperate need of a nap, but clearly *that's* not happening.

Everson fell ill two days ago, on Friday—the morning after David and Ethan left for a father-son weekend trip to Ethan's basketball tournament. Timed perfectly for the weekend when the doctor's office would be closed and I'd be alone with the two girls (how do germs know these things?), Everson's fever hit 104, prompting a harried trip to urgent care on Saturday. Once we had the fever down to a mere 100 degrees, the girls and I settled in on our comfy couch, expecting a quiet evening watching favorite movies—until, "Mommy, my tummy hurts."

When Everson's tummy ache evolved into vomiting and then a climbing fever, I propped her up on pillows next to me in bed so I could keep an eye on her all night. But as the night wore on, she drenched the sheets with perspiration and her trembling shook the bed. Frightened, I checked her temperature again—and when I saw the number 106, I froze.

And then I panicked. Only on the inside, of course. Mommies who are actors, like all mommies, must never look like they are terrified by visions of coma or meningitis as they dash for cold washcloths and ice water. We are very practiced at speaking words of comfort in soothing, calm tones while the voices in our heads are screaming, *What do I do now? Should I be calling 911? How long should I wait to see if the fever drops? Why tonight? No family, no husband, no one to help—just me and my two daughters.*

Spoiler alert: Evie lived.

How easy to joke about it today! But that night, I wasn't laughing. I felt abandoned and helpless. When Everson's trembling subsided and she drifted back to sleep, I sat in the dark and cried. I shook. I prayed, calling out to God for healing. In fact, I lay awake beside her until her little body responded to those prayers and she opened her eyes and asked for lemonade. Her fever broke, yet I prayed on all night long.

I did not pray confidently; I prayed afraid.

I did not sense God's presence; I felt alone.

Dreadfully afraid and alone. And, true confession: Angry. At God. At David. At a fallen world where illness and disease strike without warning with the power to cripple lives or take them.

Sure, today I can lightheartedly quip my spoiler alert. But every experienced mom knows this: When you face a health crisis with one of your children, *you don't know how it's going to come out.* There is no spoiler alert at the time.

And every human being who has ever suffered or loved someone who suffers knows the same. It is no joking matter when we don't know how the scene ends, is it? It's like acting out your part live on stage with no rehearsal, and suddenly discovering there's a crucial page missing from the script—the next one. Not only do you have no idea what's coming next; you have no idea how the story even ends. Facing a threatening unknown, we worry. We wonder what to do. We plead for God's intervention. We fear and even expect the worst. At least I do.

So that's why writing this book has been nothing like I envisioned. Because my plan had been to share *confidently* what I had been discovering about God's love and faithfulness since my conversion at the age of twenty-two. Here's how my original book description went: "To show through my own experience and Scripture that God loves us just as we are, just where we are, and that his healing arms embrace us in the midst of the brokenness and imperfections of our lives as he moves us toward wholeness."

And that is still my heartbeat for this book. I want to offer hope to others who have struggled as I did for so many years with such things as depression; anxiety; self-hatred; unworthiness; life-threatening eating disorders; self-harm; broken, dysfunctional upbringings; unresolved pain; emptiness; and self-destructive life patterns. There are so many who are doing what I did for far too long—projecting to others the happy veneer of the perfect life while suffering and doubting in silence and dying on the inside. Driven to look perfect, act perfect, be perfect, too many of us are embarrassed or shamed by our life choices and our negative responses to circumstances within and beyond our control. Having been there, done that, I wanted to write a book to share the hope I've found and the freedom into which I've stepped.

As an actor, a producer, and a Christian mom raising children in the long shadow of those nine towering letters—H O L L Y W O O D—I encounter women in every endeavor who struggle, like me, with the drive for perfection in the midst of a far-less-than-perfect life. I reasoned that now, tested and tried and publicly living out my faith (thanks to the success of our Pure Flix films *God's Not Dead* and *God's Not Dead 2*), God had given me a new boldness. I could declare my imperfections. I could escort readers backstage and show the not-so-pretty reality behind the camera to let them know that their flaws and imperfections and failures and embarrassments are common to us all and do not disqualify us from being used by God, but are in fact the very means by which God grows us into service.

"God uses broken people all the time to do his kingdom work, just as he always has," I've wanted to shout, "because we are all broken people! There is no one perfect but God alone. It is in our weakness that God demonstrates his strength."

Right? So that was the plan. And it was a good one, driven by mission and love and a deep sense of divine purpose.

And that is still what I want to do! There is only one problem.

I've been stuck. I opened my life script to the pages of my present days and didn't like what I read. And then there were missing pages—gaps I didn't know how to fill, because there are parts of my story God hasn't revealed to me yet. And still other parts (very unpleasant ones) that are repeated over and over, like a bad scene in the movie *Groundhog Day*.

I can't turn my unfinished, imperfect life into a book that cries perfection, because that wouldn't be the truth. But how can I address overcoming the lies of perfectionism when I'm still a hostage to them?

A SEASON OF SUFFERING

Just like Everson's tummy ache unexpectedly invaded a peaceful evening and evolved into a panic-inducing crisis, I began to write this book while thrown into a season of suffering unlike any I had ever faced. David and I had unexpectedly lost two very precious loved ones within just a few months of the release of *God's Not Dead*. Only four months before its release, David's mother died suddenly. Then our beloved Pure Flix partner and mentor Russell Wolfe, producer of *God's Not Dead*, succumbed to ALS at age fifty, just two months after the movie's release. We had been so sure that God was going to heal him on earth, yet he took him to heaven instead. Heartrending. These sudden losses at a time when we were celebrating God's surprise gift of such success stirred the still lingering grief over two others who had been taken in their prime just a few years before. David's dad had died tragically seven years earlier, meaning that neither of his sweet parents who had served the Lord as Mennonite pastors ever got to witness the success of their son's movie. And David's cousin, only nineteen years old and very close to us, died tragically in his sleep a mere four years ago.

On top of the deep grief both David and I experienced, I've been suffering the past few years with relentless physical ailments and have been diagnosed with several frightening, vague, and elusive illnesses: fibromyalgia, acute migraines, chronic fatigue syndrome, a genetic disease called porphyria, Lyme disease, and a condition called POTS (postural orthostatic tachycardia syndrome), in which the resting heart rate is very high and blood pressure extremely low, causing one to faint. Housebound for three months with this condition when I started writing this book, I had fears of dying and leaving my precious children motherless. And though I've spent thousands upon thousands of dollars on mainstream medicine, chiropractors, herbalists, and endless other medical options, I've had adverse reactions to more treatments and medications than I can count.

In light of these overwhelming symptoms, I've been striving to find a healthy balance of rest, nutrition, physical care, stress care, therapies, medications, tests and more tests, research, and of first and foremost, the Word of God and prayer, only to have to confess I haven't been able to find anything close to the healthy balance of such things. This has left me deeply discouraged.

In my year of writing this book, at times I've been too ill to drive, been unable to walk, lost vision in one eye temporarily, and even been completely bedridden at times. So I turned to some well-loved sermons from preachers of the gospel, but came up disappointed in my lack of faith. The apostle Paul writes, "For we walk by faith, not by sight" (2 Corinthians 5:7 ESV). But truth be told, when I literally could not walk, I was filled with panic, not faith.

Honesty and transparency start to get a little scary at this point, and I'm all too aware that this next confession is going to earn me some less than affirming mail from some readers, but the reality is that more than once, as I sat in the emergency room, Scripture did not comfort me at all. Hebrews 11:1 tells us, "Now faith is confidence in what we hope for and assurance about what we do not see," but that wasn't true of me, even though I wanted it to be. I didn't have a sense of confidence or assurance at all. I had doubts of God's love. I had heart-racing fear—and lots of it.

I often sat there completely alone (David was at home with the kids), and I did not have joy in the midst of suffering. I wanted to know why I was suffering so badly. I saw no signs of heavenly mercy.

Well, except for one thing. I met people there. People who were also in pain or fear or despair. I'm the kind of person who tends to strike up conversations. For instance, there was an older gentleman who just needed to have someone listen to his laundry list of medical issues. Making him laugh and finding a few things in common about our experiences relaxed him as he waited. And there was a young mom with her little boy in the ER one day. Her wide eyes and shaking voice told me her fear was powerful.

Her little boy lay limp on her shoulder, hair plastered with sweat to his forehead. We talked about kids and how hard it is to watch them suffer. How frightened we get. We both felt less alone. And then there was a teenage girl in an office all by herself. I guessed why she was there alone and stepped in to be the calming adult for a few minutes while she waited to see a doctor.

I may be exposing myself as a little dense here, but it took me a few times (not that I recommend making the ER a habitual destination) before I caught on to the fact that I *was* seeing heavenly mercy at work in those conversations, but it didn't look like the kind of mercy for which I'd been pleading. Our God is most unpredictable.

As with Everson above, at least one of our children has been ill every single week for over seven months. Between them and me, we've been in and out of emergency rooms, doctors' offices, and blood-drawing labs more times than I want to count. I've prayed the verse "by his wounds we are healed" (Isaiah 53:5), yet have found myself disappointed that illness, rather than healing, seems to dominate our home. I've prayed, spoken the Word of God, repented, rebuked, and had others pray for us—yet the onslaught of illnesses continues.

I'll stop my list here. (In my rough draft, this section went on far longer!) Don't worry; I'm not planning to spend this book complaining, nor will I fill in all the unpleasant details of illnesses. I know full well that countless people are dealing with far worse, and they would gladly accept my little list of woes in exchange for their own devastating circumstances. Terminal illness. A marriage falling apart. A son or daughter maimed in combat. A loved one arrested. An injury suffered. Victimization by some violent act. The list goes on and on. The last thing any of us need is a "who's got it worse" comparison, for there is always someone who *does* have it worse!

So here's the challenge I've been facing. While working on this book, these struggles have seemed all-consuming to me. In recent months, faced with one painful circumstance after another, I've been genuinely surprised (and downright discouraged) to discover how often I feel just as lost, just as anxious, just as insecure, just as unqualified, and just as frustrated as I did at 2:00 a.m. as I watched Everson's temperature climb—hands shaking, heart pounding. But I kept hiding it all under the veneer of the "successful" Christian life, whatever that means. I admit it: I've been profoundly disappointed in my spiritual responses and lack of knowing or comfort from God in my travails of life.

I don't know how this season of trial is going to end, or *if* it will end. Will it end in deliverance? Healing? Or more suffering? When I get to the end of this period, will I hear the words, "Well done, my good and faithful servant," reverberating over the loudspeaker? (That *seems* highly unlikely, given how I've been struggling. How could I deserve the words "well done"?) Or will I come up terribly short? (I feel like I already have!)

Will I be cut from the part I am playing in God's story? (Isn't that what I deserve?) Fired? Blacklisted? Surely there are far more qualified people to write a message—spiritual grown-ups—rather than the uncertain child I feel myself to be these days.

It's not that I hadn't expected more trials and difficulties. I get it that those are always a part of life on this earth. But I did not expect *my responses* to result in the same old struggles.

PUSHING THROUGH

As I see it, feeling as confused and defeated as I have been, I had a choice to make about this book. Either I would choose not to write it, or I would push through it anyway and see where God took me. No spoiler alert needed this time, right? You are already reading the book, so you know I pushed through, just as I've pushed through storm after storm ever since I've been saved. How do I stay close to God through such things? Where has this series of storms been coming from? Where will it lead?

You have begun reading my story, but you don't know where it's leading. And that makes us even, because neither do I.

I only know that quitting would ensure my defeat. Pushing through at least holds some possibility of my discovering the truth God wants me to know. So the book I've actually written is quite different from the one I'd planned to write. Because I've decided that rather than write from what I've *already* learned, I will write instead from *what I'm struggling to discover*. Rather than writing from victory, I'm writing from the battle-field, exposing where I'm defenseless.

Why? Because pretending I'm living in victory when I'm not will just lead me deeper into defeat. Life is hard, and I despise the veneer of faith-talk portraying that life is all good when much of it is quite bad. I can't stand frauds, so sometimes I'm so real that I walk away from conversations, thinking, *Hmm, why did I just share that?* I've been told by some that I am way too transparent. But I believe, humbly, that not pretending and being honest are gifts God has given me to help others. We truly heal from each other's stories. We can connect with each other when we confess our unanswered questions and weaknesses.

We are defenseless against our enemy if we are living a lie.

There is much I do not know, but of this I am sure: I cannot win this battle alone. I've done it alone—did it for years, in fact—to disastrous results.

I'm not going back to alone!

I'm going forward with Jesus.

And I will tell you why. Because at the risk of sounding like an old hymn, *I once was lost.* Wholly, desperately, devastatingly lost. I'd lived my life my way with no personal connection whatsoever to the God of the universe—the God who made me. And when finally, at the end of myself, I cried out in desperation, "God, if you're really there, show yourself to me"—he did. Dramatically. Personally. On the spot.

And then he began to change me.

I'm going to tell you that story. And then you'll understand why, even in the throes of my current battlefield of questions and doubts, I cannot and will not go back to life without Jesus Christ.

I take comfort in this: I know I'm not the only one on this battlefield. There are legions of us who are Christians, who love God, who follow Jesus, yet who, when brutally honest with ourselves, limp along and falter with our wounds and with the shortcomings and limits of our faith. But we try to hide it. We smile and say we are fine when we are anything but.

Simply put, even though I understand the principle that God is the finisher of my faith, I'm not as "finished" as I believe I "should be" by now.

So I decided to see what God has to say about being finished.

And since not knowing how the scene finally ends tends to cause us the most angst, I'm looking at the ultimate final scene. Jesus, hanging on the cross in the midst of an agonizing and torturous death, spoke three final words before he breathed his last: *It is finished.* Jesus finished his work. Speaking words so critically important that he chose to declare them as his final words from the cross.

We may not yet have a clear understanding of what "it is finished" means for us and our struggle. I don't yet. But we do know that Jesus declared it to be so. So let's agree that we will struggle together to discover the power these words can have in our lives today.

I want to discover how to live in peace, how to survive and thrive, how to work with God rather than against him in all the unfinished places of our lives. So I'm going to start at my beginning, back to my childhood, to an opening scene from my life. And as my story unfolds, I'm going to look for evidence of God's fingerprints all over the script of my life, even, like the scenes in the waiting room, in the midst of ugly scenes where I missed the real work that God was doing.

Chapter 3

THE CRYBABY AND
THE FRAIDYCAT

In the beginning was the Word, and the Word was with
God, and the Word was God . . . He was in the world,
and though the world was made through him, the world
did not recognize him.

JOHN 1:1, 10

"Mom, I'm home," I yelled from the front door after a fun spring day
in first grade. I didn't hear an answer, so I assumed she was putting my
three-year-old brother, Josh, down for a nap. I opened a cabinet door.

Hmmm, a Little Debbie or a Twinkie? I asked myself, scanning the
snack shelf for my favorites. Rewarding myself with the comfort of a sweet
treat every day after school was as much a part of my routine as putting
on my jammies at bedtime.

As I savored my cream-filled chocolate cupcake, I watched my older
brother, Jason, through the kitchen window. Barely home from school,
he was already on his bike, popping wheelies as he headed for our cousins'
house down our lane. *He makes wheelies look so easy*, I thought, telling
myself that was only because he was three years older than me. Just the
day before, he had goaded me into trying a wheelie, and I'd fallen and
skinned my knees. As I ran back into the house crying, his taunts of

"crybaby" rang in my ears. *Why couldn't I do anything right?* Watching him now, effortlessly sending his front wheel sailing high, the familiar feeling of never measuring up washed over me.

The phone rang, and I dashed to answer it, hoping to hear my favorite voice on the line.

"Meet ya at the fence!" Mattie said. Familiar words I loved.

"On my way," I answered. Swallowing the last of my cupcake in one gulp, I called out, "Going to Mattie's," assuming Mom could hear me, and ran for the door, leaving the phone dangling by its cord. When it smacked hard against the wall, I stopped dead in my tracks, hoping Mom hadn't heard. Silence.

I berated myself as I backtracked and gently returned the phone to its hook, and I bolted out of the kitchen, wincing again when I heard the screen door slam behind me.

As I ran across the lawn toward the long, barbed-wire-topped fence that separated Mattie's ten-acre property from the seven acres where I lived on my grandparents' land, I could see Mattie running toward me, her wavy, shoulder-length hair streaming behind her, a huge grin on her face. Though we were both six years old with sandy-blonde hair, Mattie was almost a head taller. I was skinny and short and envied that she was tall and athletic. Size and strength were definite advantages in our world, since much of the time we were surrounded by Mattie's three older brothers, my four older cousins (two of them boys), and my tall, lanky nine-year-old brother. Other than little Josh (at three, still too young to play with the rest of us), I was the smallest one—something I was reminded of all too often.

WHERE MY JOY CAME OUT

"So what do you wanna do?" Mattie asked. "Climb the tree or ride bikes?" At school recess that day, we'd begun plotting our afternoon escapades and had narrowed it down to these two favorite pastimes.

"Climb the tree. My brother and cousins are out on their bikes, and I don't want them trying to run us off the road," I said. She nodded, aware of how often I was picked on by my older brother and some assortment of my Logan cousins. Having three older brothers herself, she commiserated. But one big difference between Mattie and me—if she did get picked on (which happened to her far less often than it did to me), she spoke up for herself, and her brothers would back off. Not me. In our little world, it seemed that I was the only one who had a target on my back.

I quickly climbed the three-foot wire fence, careful to not get scratched or snagged on the row of barbed wire along the top, and landed on Mattie's grass, with the feeling I had arrived in a land where I belonged. I felt I mattered at Mattie's place in a way that I longed to matter everywhere else. I doubt I could have found words for that concept at the tender age of six, but I remember the feeling with painful clarity. I can't say, though, that my reasons for feeling that way are clear to me, even now. They aren't. All I know is that I—the sensitive little girl—often felt invisible at school and home. In my eyes, Mom always seemed busy with my baby brother or other duties; Dad's time and attention always seemed focused on work and household chores; and my brother seemed to consider me either a pest or—worse yet, when he did notice me—an easy mark for his taunts. But Mattie's place was my haven.

She and I trotted over to the dried mud puddle to admire the mud pies we'd neatly arranged a few days earlier after enjoying a warm spring rain. At least my brother and cousins showed no interest in disturbing us when we played pancake chefs at the fence.

The thought of pancakes made me think of dinner. It must have done the same for Mattie because she said, "Mom said you can come for dinner. She's making homemade bread and beef stew. And I think she's going to bake cookies too!"

I'd been hoping Mattie would invite me to her house for dinner tonight. Mrs. Moore always had the evening meal ready at five o'clock for their whole family—a rare occurrence at my house. Mattie's dad worked construction, and he and her brothers would all come to the table talking about their day while teasing and laughing. I was certain they had to be the best family dinners in our little town of Burlington, Illinois. Being at Mattie's just made my joy come out.

"I love your mom's beef stew!" My mouth watered at the very thought of the huge pot of meat, potatoes, and vegetables, simmering with lots of savory herbs and spices. And her homemade chocolate chip cookies were the best. Hanging out with Mrs. Moore felt as comforting as the kitchen time I treasured with my two grandmas, where warm memories were made. Mom's mom, Grandma Bahr, welcomed my help in her kitchen as she made her delicious German potato salad, homemade breads, fresh rhubarb pie, and Italian beef.

Grandma Logan, on my dad's side, made yummy traditional Greek cookies, the absolute best Greek salad smothered in feta cheese, olive oil, and red wine vinegar. Her delicious homemade bread inspired good-natured fights between the cousins over who got to soak their bread in the yummy leftover dressing in the bottom of the salad bowl. And the mere mention of Grandma's toast with her delicious homemade spreads made my mouth water. Obviously, comfort and food have gone hand in hand for me from my earliest memories.

Mrs. Moore's meals weren't the only things I loved about her, though. She smiled all the time, as if enjoying everything she was doing. And she did a lot—she sewed Halloween costumes and clothes for Mattie and her brothers, and she was the most incredible artist, often working on a drawing or painting. She also took Mattie and her brothers to church every week—something we did only every now and then for a special occasion. It seemed to me that everything about her was just lovely.

Unlike Mattie's dad, my father's schedule was very irregular. Dad was a policeman for Kane County—something I was very proud of—in a city far bigger than our little farming town of Burlington, so he often came home late in the evening. This meant we didn't have a regular dinnertime. I don't remember Mom and I spending much time in the kitchen, and when she did, she usually only had time to throw something together after work due to our rigorous sports schedules. I do recall her roasted chicken or chicken and rice, and of course, her green bean casserole with yucky canned onions that my brothers and I scoffed at. But at least she tried to get dinner on the table. (Today, I can relate, as I am the worst cook!)

Mattie and I reached our favorite climbing tree, which grew on our property line next to the fence on Mattie's side. Its hefty lower branches drew us upward and, mixed with a little imagination, transformed the tree into an elegant stairway in our mighty castle from which we surveyed our kingdoms.

The Logan kingdom had three houses (one for us and one each for two uncles and aunts and assorted cousins), plus a barn converted to a house where my grandparents lived. There was also a small barn where my uncle kept two horses. Our gravel lane connected all the houses on our acreage.

Mattie's kingdom had her house, a barn, and a shed her family called the Cat House, where we often played house with my cousin Stephanie, only one year older. The three of us had created our very own secret club and called ourselves the Sunflower Girls. No boys allowed!

The Moores had a trampoline too—something I enjoyed far more when bouncing only with Mattie. Otherwise, it seemed like I always got hurt. I remember wanting to do flips like my brother and cousins. One day, when I was a bit older and wore what I considered to be the nerdiest pink-framed glasses, I went for it. I worked up to a high bounce, gathered my nerve, and flipped forward. In midair, with a thrill of awe, I realized it was working—an airborne somersault! But when I landed on my feet, they bounced so hard and fast that my knees slammed into my face and right into my glasses. That graceful flip earned me a bloody gash on each side of my nose, providing my brother and cousins with an endless source of laughter. Maybe other children could take such ribbing without burning with shame, but not me. For the next few weeks, every glance in a mirror reminded me that I was a klutz and a laughingstock.

From our perch in our castle, my thin ponytail swaying in the breeze and Mattie's curls flying, we could spend hours spinning stories about the many adventures in our kingdoms, especially as we spied on the antics of our assortment of rough-and-tumble brothers and cousins. We imagined them to be soldiers defending our lands one day, and court jesters the next, often laughing ourselves silly knowing that if they were to hear our impressions of them, we'd be dethroned in a heartbeat. It was such fun to have my best friend living right next door and an entire kingdom for playing hide-and-seek, riding bikes, drawing masterpieces in the dirt, and enjoying other such favorite antics. Time with Mattie always flew by too quickly.

"Girls!" Mrs. Moore called from her front door. Her call felt like the "welcome home" I longed for. I didn't know exactly why or how to explain it, but I always felt I was home with Mattie and her family, like they were my second family.

I imagined that I could actually see the scent of warm cookies (just like in cartoons) floating from the oven and out the open door, past Mrs. Moore, right through the front yard and up into our tree. She didn't need to call me twice!

"Andrea, I'm so glad you could come. You girls go wash up now." As Mattie's mom scurried from oven to stovetop to table, I watched her every move. The sound of her voice was gentle and cheerful, and I drank in her every word, beaming when she thanked us for helping to set the table. With Mrs. Moore, I always felt *seen*.

Mr. Moore took his usual seat at the head of the table, and then Mrs. Moore said grace. We didn't do that at our house, but I loved it when she prayed—which felt just like she was talking to a friend, as if God himself were in the room with us. I'd never heard anyone else do that. As soon as she said "amen," everyone was reaching for bowls of food at once and talking over everybody else and having a good time being together. By the time we'd all helped clear the table, I knew I needed to head home, though I didn't want to leave. Everything about being there made me glow inside. Well, except for all the sneezing. I was severely allergic to their dogs.

"You have a good night," Mrs. Moore said as she kneeled and gave me a wink good-bye. "Mattie, are you going to walk Andrea to the fence?" But she and Mattie and I all knew she didn't really have to ask. That's what we always did.

Once I was back on my own lawn and approaching my kitchen door, I felt a familiar uncomfortable comparison creeping into my heart.

"I'm home," I called out as I stepped inside. But it didn't feel like home.

"Okay," Mom's voice called from her bedroom. "Time to get ready for bed." My sense of comparison grew stronger as I headed down the hallway to brush my teeth and put on my pajamas. Why didn't my mother watch over me the way Mattie's mother did with her? Why didn't she stand by to make sure I brushed my teeth right? Or give me snuggles after I got my jammies on? I wanted my mother to sit on my bed after I had crawled under the covers, to talk to me in a soft musical voice and stroke my hair like the moms in TV shows. I wanted to feel like she was enjoying me, liked she loved just being together. Instead, I felt oddly alone. At the tender age of six, it seemed to me (rightly or wrongly) that I was on my own.

I suppose many children compare the families of their friends with their own and find that their own come up short, but there is no doubt that to me, simply spending time at the Moore's place was the ultimate in belonging, while by comparison mine seemed lacking. No doubt that says a lot more about the little girl I was—my needs, longings, and emotional makeup, than it does about my parents' love and care, for today I know they loved me then and love me still. But for whatever complex set of reasons, I often felt invisible—unheard and unnoticed—as if I didn't much matter.

STICKS AND STONES . . . AND WORDS

I awoke the next morning, a Saturday, to a loud thumping in the living room. Curious, I trotted out to see.

"Get out of the way, you dummy," my older brother yelled.

"Hey, Andy," Dad said (how I loved it when he used his special nickname for me), "Move out of the way. We're rolling up the carpet to take it out the door."

"How come?" I asked.

"Because, stupid, we're having the floors redone." Jason's sarcastic tone caught my dad's attention.

"Jason," Dad said in a displeased tone, but nothing more. I wished my brother would get in trouble for calling me names, but usually he got away with it.

I get it that whoever coined the rhyme *sticks and stones may break my bones, but words will never hurt me* was trying to teach children to not be wounded by cruel words, but it never worked for me. Of course, poking fun and bantering insults is a common behavior among siblings, but even so, being the victim of name-calling hurt my heart terribly. I was wired to be especially sensitive.

Stupid. Crybaby. Weakling. Wimp. Fraidycat. All were labels I was internalizing without knowing the damage they were doing. Did I sometimes argue back or complain about them? Yes. There were times I balled my hands into fists and tried to strike back, but my feeble attempts were simply laughed off. I'd unleash my tongue and scold and threaten to tell Mom or Dad and demand an apology, but my words had no effect. And over time, all the names added up in my mind to mean I was *never enough*. Not strong enough or smart enough or brave enough or good enough. Inferior. Loser. And deep inside, I believed it. I saw myself as the weak one. *Why would anyone want me around anyway?*

Several hours later, I was outside under two huge pine trees, where my dad and brother had placed the giant roll of carpeting. One of my older cousins was goofing around with me and suddenly announced a grand idea: "I'll get my ATV and jump it!"

"Ummm . . . huh?" I stammered, foreseeing disaster, as this cousin was fearless. I felt a lump grow in my throat at the very thought of it.

Each of our three families owned a three-wheel ATV. As my cousin ran to get his, my tummy clenched in nervousness. He was such a daredevil. *Maybe I should go in the house now*, I thought to myself. But I didn't want to look like a coward or be called Fraidycat again. Vacillating, I waited too long. He pulled up next to me, revving his engine.

"Come on! Get on, Annie! Climb on behind me," he said. Then seeing the fear in my face, he taunted me. "You wuss! You aren't afraid, are you?"

"No. I just want to watch," I said lamely. But I *was* afraid. I had a sinking feeling that something bad was about to happen. I looked around, hoping one of my parents or uncles or aunts would see us and put a stop to the madness. No such luck.

"Aw, don't be such a sissy. You aren't going to be a crybaby, are you? Get on! Hurry up."

Again I said no. But his taunts cut me to the core. Finally, mad that I didn't see a way out of it without being mocked, I said, "Fine." Heart pounding, I climbed on behind him. He revved the engine. I closed my eyes. Suddenly we were speeding forward, and my eyes sprang open, afraid *not* to see what was coming. We were headed directly toward the giant roll of carpet, picking up speed. I wanted to scream for him to stop, but I couldn't find my voice. I opened my mouth and tried—but no sound came out.

I felt my cousin yank back on the handlebars as he revved the engine. The front of the ATV lifted, but not enough. The front wheel skimmed the top of the carpet roll, and I felt my body lifting off the bike and flying forward into the air, flipping head over heels. I landed with a thump, flat on my back on the carpeting, with the wind knocked out of me and unable to breathe. Then, to my horror, I saw the front wheel of the ATV, still airborne, coming straight down toward me, my cousin's face peering down over his handlebars, his eyes wide with terror. Unable to move or scream, I lay helpless as the weight of the ATV landed on my chest, crossing over me from left to right.

For just a moment as it hit me, everything seemed stuck in slow motion. Pain paralyzed me. The ATV paused as my cousin tried to throw his weight backward to reduce the impact, but still it lurched forward over me, followed by the back two tires rolling over my chest and thighs.

I still couldn't breathe. All I felt was weight, pain, and terror. I heard the screams of my cousin, but they sounded distant. I feared I was dying. Was I crushed? Was I bleeding? Were my lungs going to explode? Finally came a gasp of air. And that's when my screams finally escaped their prison. Believing I was dying, I screamed with all my might.

My screams so pierced the air that my mother, visiting my dad's parents two houses down our lane, heard me, tore out of their home, and sprinted across two acres. Then she was by my side, touching my chest and checking my arms and legs—and still my screams did not stop. As she examined me, I saw her anxiety begin to melt away, and with it my screams melted into sobs and then quieted into whimpers.

I have no memory of what happened next. Someone must have carried me home and put me in bed. But I do remember lying on my bed later that evening, alone in my room, and wondering, *Why don't they take me to the hospital? How do they know I'm okay—that I don't have a broken bone or something squashed inside of me? Am I okay? Am I safe? Why is no one with me?*

I would think the memory of my mother sprinting to my side and breathlessly checking over me would have assured my six-year-old heart that she loved me deeply. Today, I see her love clearly. As a mother myself, I can fully appreciate the terror she must have felt for me and the waves of relief that washed over her to see that her daughter was safe. Yet my child-size heart, instead, ended that frightening day wondering all the more if I was truly loved.

Was I truly *alone* in my own home? Did I lack for attention and affection? Is that why I loved to be at Mattie's? Was I really the targeted child in the family, bullied by my older brother and cousins? I can't answer those questions with any certainty. But I can be sure of two things. First, in my formative years I *believed* I was all that and more. I *saw* myself as less than and as unworthy. I *believed* I was a disappointment. I felt alone. Rejected. Unlovable. Unprotected. And with good reason or not, that is the image of myself I carried forward. It was an image that would continue for many years before it would shatter. Then even more time would pass before I could even begin to replace it with a new image.

Second, I do know now that my parents loved me then and love me to this day. And I believe that they as parents did what I do every day with my own children; they did their best to be good parents in the midst of lives filled with challenges and demands that I, as a little girl, knew nothing about. They did it imperfectly, just as I do, for none of us are perfect. In fact, I wouldn't change my past. It made me who I am today. And now that I'm a parent, I am able to hold a mirror to my own weaknesses and take my brokenness to God, who always graciously says that tomorrow is a new day.

Today, this imperfect daughter of Jim and Linda Logan treasures the image of Mom running to my aid, just as I treasure memories of my Dad's protective care, which you'll read about later. These are images of love and protection, a foretaste of God—the perfect parent who would in a few years come running to his wayward, broken daughter.

Chapter 4

THAT GIRL

For we do not have a high priest who is unable to empa-
thize with our weaknesses, but we have one who has been
tempted in every way, just as we are—yet he did not sin.
Let us then approach God's throne of grace with confidence, so that we may receive mercy and find grace to
help us in our time of need.

HEBREWS 4:15–16

Mrs. Humes, my fourth-grade teacher, walked up and down between the neat rows of our school desks, placing one copy of the test on each desk. "Please do not pick up your pencils until I tell you to," she said.

The closer she got to me, the harder my heart pounded. I hated tests. This year more than ever. Last year, if I studied very hard, I could earn A's and B's, but I'd never been satisfied with that. I expected straight A's of myself. This year was even worse. Everything about geography seemed beyond my grasp, especially this unit on reading maps. I'd paid attention, studied my textbook, and struggled through my homework, but I still wasn't getting it.

Her black pumps clicked closer on the gray tile floor until I saw them next to the desk in front of me. I didn't look up as she approached my desk. I liked Mrs. Humes. She was kind to me and often smiled and laughed throughout the day. But this day, I was afraid that if I looked up into her kind eyes, I might cry, so I kept my head down, as if studying my hot-pink high tops. She placed my test facedown in front of me. I looked at the stapled corner. Oh, no—four pages! I tried to swallow, but my mouth went dry.

Finally, her crisp voice broke the silence. "You may begin. You have thirty minutes."

I flipped it over. The very first page was a map of the United States, with a list of instructions and questions down the right-hand side. I flipped through the entire test, each page more intimidating than the one before. I heard pencils hit papers, the rustle of pages, the tapping of fingers and shuffling of feet, but nothing was as loud as the throbbing of my heart in my ears. I wrote my name on the designated line and tried to make sense of the first question, but I froze. It just wasn't registering. Finally, with a deep breath of panic mixed with resignation, I scrawled a big F across the top. Next to it I wrote, "I suck. I suck. I suck." Then I put my head down on the desk.

It wasn't surprising that on my report card that semester, Mrs. Humes's neat penmanship declared, "Andrea often defeats herself before she starts."

Little did she know she'd just summed up most of my efforts at life from then through adolescence. In my first eight years, I'd come to see myself through the faulty filter of *never enough*. From the age of nine onward, I struggled with how to be myself when I didn't much like who I saw myself to be. Mrs. Humes was on to something that would take me years to discover: when we see ourselves as unworthy and of little or no value, our actions follow suit. I was on my way to becoming a champion of self-destruction.

FAMILY TREASURES, FRAGILE SPIRIT

It's not that everything in my next few years was doom and gloom. Far from it. Living in my small rural town, surrounded by farms and family and friends, I experienced many idyllic moments. I loved extended family celebrations on holidays and birthdays, with tables overflowing with yummy food made by my grandmas on both sides of the family. Dad's side, the Logans, were Greek, and they enchanted us with holiday treats like bloodred Easter eggs, baklava, and Greek lemon rice chicken soup called Avgolemono soup. Gram Logan's Greek salad always had the perfect ratio of red wine vinegar, olive oil, and Greek herb dressing. I especially loved cookies (made from scratch, of course), including her gingerbread men.

And what a blast to pile into Gram and Grandpa's RV for a family camping trip, where even rainy days were fun, thanks to hours of boisterous card games and Grandpa's "let me tell you kids" political rants that made us laugh, even though we were clueless about what he was talking about. One favorite memory of Gram was the time in third grade when I fell into a mud puddle at lunchtime. Gram showed up at school with a change of clothes. She was always there for me when I needed her.

Grandma and Grandpa Bahr's German home was just as delightful. Grandpa was a cuddlebug, and Grandma a wiz in the kitchen and the vice president of the local bank! In preparation for the holidays, we would bake batches of cookies, along with Mom and her sister, my aunt Donna. I loved dropping the light, flaky, flowery rosettes in oil, sprinkling them with powdered sugar, and then molding the spritz from the cookie press to form little Christmas trees. My little brother Josh and I especially loved to press our thumbprints into the cookie dough and drop food coloring into frosting for our own custom colors. We probably ate more cookies than our body weight. All the while, Jason would be helping Grandpa Bahr chop wood for the ever-toasty wood burning stove downstairs. And such wonderfully warm memories of decorating the Christmas tree and horsing around with our family.

Yet despite those wonderful joys, I never seemed to shake the sadness of the fragile image of myself as inferior and invisible. Today I see all the evidence to the contrary—that I *did* matter to those I loved, but I was blind to it, believing it was only they who were special, not I.

As I grew, I felt less and less comfortable in my own skin. My constant battles with eczema and allergies, complete with puffy eyes, runny nose, and sneezes, certainly didn't help. I was either drugged on Benadryl, leaving me too tired to keep up, or fighting through the discomfort just to be a normal kid like everyone around me. When I was kept inside, looking out through windows as brothers and cousins played outside, it was as if I had a recording inside my head playing the same tired message over and over: *Why can't I just be normal? I'm a misfit and different from the other kids.* When I did play, just like in my primary years, I was still the youngest and smallest, and the slowest or the most likely to be injured. Always, it seemed to me, I was the butt of jokes and teasing. And thanks to the glasses I needed by fourth grade (clear pink rims that I was so embarrassed to wear), along with braces for my buck teeth a few years later, the labels Four Eyes, Brace Face, and Bucky Beaver didn't do much for the self-image of a girl who already felt like she got the short end of the stick.

In contrast, my mother was stunning. I was in awe of her beauty and would stare at her as she applied her makeup and set her hair with hot rollers in the morning. One of my memories is going to her aerobics class and watching as she, sporting her Jane Fonda-like leotard, did jumping jacks and leg lifts. And a laughable memory was that of Grandma Bahr giving Mom and me look-alike perms.

Aunt Donna was a skilled seamstress. Several times for special-occasion gifts, she made me lovely hand-sewn dresses. In awe of owning something so lovely, I'd run my fingers over the delicate stitching, darling fabric, and the sweet little fabric flowers stitched onto the neckline. But when it came time to get dressed for a special holiday service at the local Methodist church, I'd change my clothes again and again. Standing before the mirror wearing a pretty dress from Aunt Donna, I'd see looking back at me an ugly girl with a bowl haircut framing an ugly face. I'd take the dress off and try on the next and be disappointed once again. Meanwhile, my mother, having grown impatient with my indecision, would get frustrated—as would any mother wanting to get out the door to church on time. Poor Mom. She wasn't wired like me emotionally and never seemed to know how to deal with my sensitivities.

Now that I have my own children, one of my daughters is cut from the same mold as me, and I see how sensitive her spirit is. Each child is wired very differently, and with God's help I'm learning patience as a mother myself at how to nurture each child's needs.

I realize that many kids have these same types of experiences and come through them just fine, but for whatever reason, by the time I was nine, I had internalized the insults and failures, the weaknesses and comparisons, and considered myself unworthy of acceptance and affection. If you had asked me at the time to define *unworthy*, I wouldn't have been able to. But I was doing a pretty good job living it.

I experimented with a variety of ways to find my voice in relationships. Playing with Barbie dolls with my cousins, Stephanie and Shelly, often led to the usual childhood squabbles over who got to play with the newest dolls or the best clothes. I tried my hand at arguing for the best, but (as is often true of the youngest) I couldn't bear to hold my own against their displeasure, and I grew afraid to speak up for myself. So I always got the leftovers. Once I had a crush on a boy in class named Kyle. I was so excited one day to discover that Kyle had a crush on me as well, and I couldn't wait to tell a friend about it. But she was not happy to hear it because she, too, liked Kyle. The next day at school, she made up a lie about me and told the whole class. For a week no one liked me. I cried and cried for days and then told her, "Fine! You can have Kyle."

Silly memories of childhood spats? Maybe. But I still recall the sting of feeling betrayed by someone I trusted, yet caving in because I couldn't bear the disapproval or that gut-wrenching feeling of being abandoned by my friends. Even what people called me was chosen by others rather than by me. Dad called me Andy (his special name for me that I loved), while Mom called me Ann or Andrea; my brothers—Ann; and my aunts, uncles, and cousins—Annie. Friends just took their pick. It never occurred to me to tell others what I wanted to be called.

I know I'm not alone in these experiences. I meet women from many walks of life who share their own versions of this story.

I had become *that* girl. The one who is easy to bully, unworthy of loyalty, deserving of being betrayed, too timid to stand up for herself.

And yet I was reaching a significant turning point—not overnight, but gradually.

How did the girl who believed herself not good enough, whose default survival mode had been to not rock the boat so that she wouldn't be disparaged or mocked or left abandoned, gather the will to find a fighting spirit? I'm not sure, but I did, and I think sports was part of the answer.

My mom had taken me as an energetic child of three to ballet lessons, which I loved and participated in enthusiastically for about three years. Later, we added gymnastics and tumbling. Then during my school years, I loved sports (as long as I wasn't playing with my big brother and cousins), and in that arena at least, I had the heart of a competitor—probably thanks to being mocked and made fun of. Volleyball, basketball, soccer, softball—I did them all. Was I a shining star on the court or field? No. In truth, I was only fair. I worked hard and did my part and then looked longingly at the girls who were recognized for excellence. How I wanted to shine—at something, at *anything*.

I was average. But average wasn't *perfect*. I was good. But good wasn't *good enough*. Was this a message I heard from my parents or coaches? Not that I recall. It was the internal voice of a girl who believed she never measured up and therefore lacked worth. That voice, left unchallenged for years, laid down deep roots in the core of my soul. Even to this day, those old, deeply buried seeds sometimes sprout up, trying to wreak havoc on my identity.

But good enough or not, my internal satisfaction at playing sports and successfully being part of a team, of feeling myself improve and belong, of having some shining moments even if I was not the shining star, fanned the flame of the competitor inside me. I became a diehard athlete—a girl who had pictures of Michael Jordan on her wall and loved everything about sports. And that awoke the spirit of the fighter in me, at least in some areas of my life.

For instance, by the age of nine, I had already proved I was self-sufficient. If Mom couldn't make time for me, then I would take care of myself. And if she wasn't going to fix Josh and me after-school snacks, then I'd fix our snacks myself. And if my parents weren't going to gather round the dinner table like Mattie's family did, then I'd heat up some frozen burritos or Top Ramen, and Josh and I would sit down together and watch TV.

The girl who had put the F on her own paper, who had played willingly with the leftover dolls, and had given up Kyle—the one who had been so afraid to be mocked and ostracized by her cousins that she became the landing pad for a flying ATV—that girl ended up teetering on the edge of defeat. What would I do about it? I didn't yet know. But something.

One of my uncles coached basketball for elementary school kids. I joined the team in fourth grade and loved the sport. As in other sports, I wasn't bad—and wasn't great. During practice, I always worked hard, but when game time came, my uncle nearly always kept me on the bench. I wanted so badly to play. As game after game came and went, I sat on the bench, thinking, *Why don't my parents come and stick up for me?* I couldn't imagine speaking up for myself. I rarely felt comfortable speaking to adults or even making eye contact with them. To risk conflict with my coach? Unthinkable. I just assumed I was powerless to bring about change.

Fortunately, my coaches for soccer, softball, and volleyball (my favorite) did play me, so in every season, sports were a huge positive part of my life. Oddly, at the same time, sports reinforced my belief that I was never excellent in anything. Like Mrs. Humes, my coaches and teammates often told me I was too hard on myself. "Lighten up. Stop beating yourself up. Give yourself a break." But how could I? I saw my life through a lens of criticism when all I wanted was to be perfect.

In the long run, however, it would be my family life more than sports that eventually awakened my fighter instinct the most.

BROKEN CONNECTIONS

I'm not sure at what age I began to catch on that our home life lacked a healthy sense of connection. Certainly not as a very young child. I have a clear memory of a very connected moment when, at three years old, I was tested in the allergist's office and pricked all over by little needles. Mom gave me her hand and told me to squeeze every time it hurt, and I squeezed with all my might. She was my physical lifeline that day, and I knew she loved me. And then there's the memory of my dad putting on his Lionel Richie records and dancing all over the living room, snapping his fingers while chomping on a Granny Smith apple (his favorite) as I watched and giggled. And like so many little girls, I have warm memories of pretending to fall asleep to the TV so that Daddy would carry me up to bed. I'm grateful.

Despite those few standout memories, however, I don't recall a great deal of playfulness and physical affection that included my parents, especially not between each other. I had noticed by first grade that everyone at Mattie's home related to one another far more than my family did, but I assumed then that Mattie's family was just special. At that age, it didn't occur to me that perhaps something was broken in the Logan household. But by the time I was in fifth grade, I was catching on that my mom and dad didn't connect much with each other, much less with me and my older brother, Jason. Somehow, Josh, as the youngest, managed to get more attention from everyone. I remember feeling that I was mostly raising myself, and over time, as my mother's attention for Josh also began to fade, I began to take on the mothering role in his life.

I have no memory of my family ever sitting at our kitchen table at the same time with all of us laughing, or even talking, not even on weekends. True, like many busy families, at least one of us kids was often at practice or a sporting event. And since Dad usually worked late and Mom's hours flexed, more often than not, we heated and ate meals at different times. Mom kept foods in the pantry or freezer that were easy for us to heat up, so that when she didn't cook, we could fend for ourselves. And I recall rather bizarre combinations of foods thrown together at the last minute, such as something we called bunsteads—an egg, mayo, and tuna mixture spread on a hamburger bun with a slab of cheese and then toasted. (Ewww!)

If you've picked up on the fact that my memories of love and food are deeply connected, you are right—as you will see in the years to come. Interestingly, I recall being so impressed with the lunches that Mattie's mom packed for her to take to school that I asked Mom to do the same. She did it a time or two, and it meant so much to me that I was afraid to eat the whole sandwich. I was afraid that if I did, her love would be gone.

By the time I hit puberty, I remember catching on that many of my friend's moms had talked to them about how their bodies would change, but my mother had never explained sexual development or the act of sex to me. I was often bewildered or alarmed at the changes in my body and had only the sketchy information I'd gained at school and the highly questionable whispers among my friends to rely on. I felt left out not to be learning these things from my own mother, though in retrospect, I suspect I had lots of friends in the same predicament.

If not overtly affectionate, however, my mom was a very hard worker. She began cleaning houses part-time when I was about three. By the time I was ten, she took on a full-time job as a secretary. That was when I began noticing some unsettling changes in Mom's behavior—especially as she began hanging out with new friends who weren't part of our lives or Dad's.

Dad, too, was a hard worker, and I was very proud he was a policeman. I did worry, though, that he didn't seem happy in his work. I sensed sadness in him and emotional distance. It's not that he avoided relating to me; I just struggled to figure out how to relate to him. Due to his schedule, he was seldom able to attend my games or to spend time playing with me. When he was home, he spent his time doing household and outdoor chores, a world he seemed to share more with Jason than with me—a fact I envied, as I often longed for more time with him, though it seemed always beyond my reach.

When I was in sixth grade, Dad got a new job with the Food and Drug Administration. The office was in downtown Chicago, and he commuted to Geneva and took a train downtown. The schedule was grueling, but we all could tell he liked his new job far better.

One day, he came home with news he was clearly excited about. The FDA had offered him a transfer to Albuquerque, New Mexico. I could sense the tension as Mom and Dad discussed it. At first Mom was resistant, but after a few days, she said, "Yes, yes. You go on and get a place for us. We'll wait until the house sells and follow you out there." So Dad got an apartment in Albuquerque. Immediately I missed him terribly. His absence left a gaping hole in my life. I thought of him often and longed to have him back. I would spend hours writing him poems.

But I had a nagging suspicion that Mom, regardless of what she had said, had no intention of moving. For years, I'd heard one recurring disagreement between my parents that had always unsettled me. My dad often spoke wistfully of moving west. Mom, on the other hand, declared she would never move. She had been born only a few miles from where we lived in Burlington, and that's where she wanted to stay. Now with Dad's new job, I feared the worst.

Then one day when I was twelve, my dad was home from Albuquerque for the weekend, and my parents took Jason, Josh, and me to a Chinese restaurant. I wondered what special occasion we were celebrating—but even more, I wondered why neither Mom or Dad were smiling. Sometime between my plate of noodles with veggies and the delivery of my fortune cookie, my parents delivered the devastating words every child fears: "We are getting a divorce." I came home from dinner wearing a new label: that girl from the broken family. Over and over I asked myself the same question in a variety of ways: *What did I do wrong?*

Chapter 5

THE REPUTATION

"Do not be afraid; you will not be put to shame.
Do not fear disgrace; you will not be humiliated.
You will forget the shame of your youth
and remember no more the reproach of your
widowhood."

ISAIAH 54:4

Every woman who has ever parented or loved a teenage girl will understand when they read these next two chapters that there is one person on this earth for whom they will be the most painful to read—my mother. So it's vitally important that I momentarily skip ahead to this future scene—my mother saying to me, "Andrea, I can't wait to read your book. I want one of the very first copies." And she will have it, wrapped in love and tied with a commitment between daughter and mother to embrace the truth that we all live perfectly unfinished lives. My mother has long since asked forgiveness for these years, and I've long since given it. Consider the healing that must have transpired, therefore, between these incidents and the writing of this book. For today, I know beyond a doubt that I will always love her with all my heart and that I value beyond words that her heart—one of the most sensitive hearts I know—will have a bond with my children. I will never grow out of wanting my mama in my life!

◦ ⚜ ◦

At the time of that fateful Chinese dinner, my brother Jason was sixteen. Suddenly, with the divorce announced and my dad back in Albuquerque, my mom drastically changed her parenting style with my older brother. Jason, a popular sophomore, had a girlfriend who was a senior, and soon most of his friends were seniors as well. Drinking and carousing were quite open among teens in our town, and to my amazement, Mom started allowing Jason and his friends to party at our house—and she allowed them to have alcohol.

These were not quiet little parties. They were loud, with music blaring late into the night—with Mom's approval. I was astounded. I would walk through the living room on my way to the kitchen, stepping over kids passed out drunk and seeing couples making out in dark corners. I felt humiliated to be *that* family—the one with the reputation, the one scowled at by other parents at school games. My mom, on the other hand, seemed to glory in her newfound identity as "the cool mom." *How can she do this to us?* I'd agonize as I sat in the bleachers, blushing at the scathing looks thrown her way.

THE WISH TO DISAPPEAR

Over the next year, things went from bad to worse. Always a beautiful woman, Mom's wardrobe began to change. Her clothes got much tighter—distractingly, embarrassingly tight. She took on a flirtatious air with men—even divorced dads of some of my classmates at school events—which made me want to hide. Then Mom began to date, and men began dropping by, clearly flirting with her. She flirted back. Soon she was staying out late. My shame deepened. But the fighter in me stepped up.

I decided to play the grown-up. If Mom wasn't home by five, I'd call her. She made excuses that she had errands to run or needed to stop at the hospital to see a friend. I suspected they were lies and challenged her truthfulness. But my challenges were useless. Her behavior did not change.

We had a very small school—my entire class was about 140 kids—so news traveled fast. One day, I got a call from Mrs. Stevens, the mother of a girl I considered a friend. She and her brothers went to my school.

"Where is your mother?" Mrs. Stevens said.

"She's visiting so-and-so in the hospital," I said nervously, worrying why she was asking.

"No, she's not. She's—" And Mrs. Stevens launched into a very ugly description of what she claimed my mom was doing at that moment. "Your mom is a whore," she said. "Do you want to be like her? Because she's running around with my husband." (Only her words weren't quite that sanitized.) She hung up, and I felt the burning heat of blood rushing to my face. I ran to my room and buried my head in my pillow, wishing desperately I could disappear.

Over the next few months, Mrs. Stevens continued to leave hundreds of profane messages on our answering machine. Traumatized, I developed a fear of picking up the phone and answering the door.

Even more awkward, Mrs. Stevens's daughter was on my basketball team, so there would be no avoiding her. I remember being on the court trembling, nauseous at what seemed to be the knowing glares of other parents in the bleachers. *How could I ever show my face at school again?* But I did. I fought through the humiliation. I showed up for classes and games just the same.

The shame I felt over my mother's behavior, and the anger that came with it, was finding fertile soil in the layers of *not good enough* already blanketing my soul. *That* girl from *that* family was unworthy of anything good, it seemed to me. I'd had a crush on a boy in my class, Dylan, since eighth grade. Now in ninth grade, I looked on as he seemed to have a crush on everyone else but me. One shame mingled with another.

My brother Jason's activities at seventeen added to the broken identity

I was developing. One night when out carousing with friends, he joined them in spray-painting private property. He was caught, arrested, and expelled. Without my brother at school, I felt more abandoned and shamed than ever.

The ages of twelve through fourteen had been a terribly confusing and painful time. Within the span of three short years, in addition to grieving the moving away of my dad, the divorce of my parents, my mother's reputation, and my brother's expulsion, I no longer wanted to be *seen*, as I'd longed for at age six; now I desperately wanted to be invisible. The weight of shame over my family seemed too heavy to bear.

DESPERATE MEASURES

I'll handle everything myself, I thought. I was already used to coming home to an empty house and fixing Josh, now ten, an after-school snack and then watching television while munching on goodies with him. Dinnertime, never having been a reliable part of our lives, now became nonexistent. Later in the evening, when Josh or I would get hungry enough, I'd pop frozen burritos into the microwave, or we'd eat Pop-Tarts and chips. Junk food, candy, and soda were always there for the taking with no restrictions, and Josh and I, like any other normal kids, weren't inclined to restrict ourselves. Soon, a new pattern formed. Food became my single most constant comfort. If I wasn't at school or sports practice, more and more often, I was sitting in front of the TV, snacking.

With Dad gone, I believed I needed to be self-sufficient. *It's up to me*, I told myself. And yet I wasn't a grown-up and had no idea what a grown-up response would be. So I chose the most drastic thing I could think of.

"Where are you going?" I asked, the next time Mom headed out in the evening after work.

"I have to visit a friend who's sick," she said—an excuse she gave frequently.

"No, you're not," I said. "You're going out to see some man. You're lying to me!"

She dismissed me. "Whatever," she said.

"Not 'whatever'!" I yelled. "Listen to me. I'm going to be dead when you come back, Mom. I'm going to kill myself." Sure, I was feeling all the drama of puberty and hormones. I felt ignored by the people I thought were supposed to love me and care for me. But I was also feeling genuine desperation.

She stopped and looked at me. "Don't say that. It's ridiculous," she said finally.

There were so many ways she could have responded. She could have stayed home. She could have said, "Okay, we need to sit down and talk," or "Let's go for counseling." But I see now that she had no better of an idea how to handle my crisis than she did her own.

Out the door she went.

Nearing fifteen, I had friends who were using marijuana, so I joined in. It seemed harmless. Besides, I liked the feeling of belonging that came with hanging out with cool people who seemed to care about me. People who were mellow and chill. And I *did* need to chill, because more family drama would soon come swirling around me.

Dad, surprisingly, moved back to Illinois to work at the main FDA office. He lived closer to Chicago than to us, but he arranged for visits on weekends. I soon realized he was heartbroken over my mother and wanted to get back together with her. Still dating around, she wasn't interested. My anger at her intensified.

Next, Mom moved us out of the house on Burlington Road, the house we'd lived in for so long, and into a tiny house on Main Street—the only kind of house she could afford now that she was divorced. I could find nothing positive about the place. The house wasn't just small; it was shabby and dirty. Mom never cleaned anymore, so if I wanted the house clean, I had to clean it myself. If Josh and I wanted clean clothes, I was the one who did the laundry. Mom ignored the cat's litter box as well. My dad had always been an organizer and very tidy—something I always appreciated about him. Now I took organization to a whole new level. Since we lived in a pigsty and I was the only one to muck it out, I craved order, so I created it. I became a neat freak.

Jason enrolled at a high school in Elgin—about thirty minutes from Burlington. When I finished ninth grade, he graduated and soon moved to Arizona to live with our aunt and uncle and attend community college. (He then went on to Arizona State University.) Part of me envied his escape, while the other part grieved one more abandonment. I missed him.

Mom received child support from Dad, and although she seemed to have mentally and emotionally checked out of our family, one area she always came through in was financially. Still a hard worker, she often held two jobs—working auctions on weekends and being a secretary during the week—to ensure we'd never be without food or decent clothes. Even so, because we couldn't afford new, brand-name clothes, we had hand-me-downs from our cousins. But Mom always made sure my brothers and I had new shoes for sports. She also attended our sporting events. I saw this as one of the ways she showed her love. She never missed a game, which meant the world to me.

By the time I was a sophomore, my marijuana usage had expanded to alcohol and experimentation with a few more drugs. I was still hanging around with the same group of friends and just followed along with whatever they did. We were all drinking and doing drugs by that time.

I dated a senior that year, Cole, who was captain of the football team, voted homecoming king, and the guy who took me to the prom—all significant in the life of a high school girl. He was probably my first real boyfriend, though I hadn't forgotten my old crush on Dylan. Evidently, this was the first year I was cool enough for my long-awaited romance with Dylan, because after my popularity as Cole's date, Dylan asked me out. I even was chosen as the sophomore girl for the homecoming court.

Sophomore year marked another "first" that felt to me like an important milestone. I went on my first diet—a diet that Mom and I followed together. I became painfully aware that on our volleyball team, everyone but me had flat stomachs. When we would practice, in an effort to cool ourselves down, we'd pull our T-shirts up and tie them in knots, But I didn't have the nice, flat stomach many of the girls had—I had a pooch. That was one of the first times I remember being insecure about my weight. Was I fat? No—at five foot five, I weighed probably 118 pounds. But I told Mom I wanted a flat stomach. Mom was on a cantaloupe and cottage cheese diet at the time. I asked her about it, and soon we were dieting together. I thought it was pretty cool that Mom and I finally had something we could share.

But it was my junior year that ultimately proved to be the most pivotal year for me for several reasons. First, on a very positive note, I became a cheerleader, a role that tapped into my strengths and built my confidence. I had a blast as a vital part of that team.

Second, as if trying to snatch away that joy, I had a coach (of one of my other teams) that year who intensified my self-consciousness about my body. He would line us up under the pretext of inspecting our uniforms and then slowly walk down the line, eyeing us up and down. One day, when passing me, his eyes lingered on my chest. "Nice rack." I didn't dare respond, but just hearing his tone of voice made me feel like I needed a shower. I had wanted to capture his attention through hard work and strong playing. The message he was sending me was that it was my body, not my ability, that won his attention—a message played out in my future more times than I can count.

Third, not only did my drug use continue, but I dropped acid that year. I did so for my second time the night before Thanksgiving, which we were celebrating at my grandparents' house. There I was, sitting at my sweet Grandma and Grandpa Bahr's good Lutheran Thanksgiving table, high as a kite, feeling like I was floating out of my body. I couldn't even hold my head up. Luckily, they had no idea—or so I assumed. Josh was also experimenting with drugs at that point, as we had free rein to do what we wished. I felt badly that I wasn't trying to keep him away from drugs, but I couldn't blame Josh, understanding that we were both trying to dull the pain in our lives and had no role models who spoke truth and direction into us. *Who was I to try to keep him straight?*

This same year, I also "fell" into shoplifting, like I fell into dropping acid and eating mushrooms and smoking marijuana—for no other reason than that all my friends were doing it. I'd started it with my girlfriends at a local Target where some of them worked. I stole silly things—flip-flops, bras, underwear, and tops—just whatever. It was easy, and the adrenaline rush gave me a jolt, feeling powerful in a world that often left me feeling so powerless.

And sadly, my junior year was also the year I surrendered my virginity. *Better that*, I reasoned that first night, *than risk losing this guy to some girl who will.*

Then finally, at the end of my junior year, came the ultimate trigger that would propel me into even more destructive decisions.

One day, Mom stepped into the living room while I was watching TV and with great happiness announced, "I'm marrying Bob! I'm moving to Springfield."

Shock reverberated through me.

I threw the remote control across the room, and it slammed into the wall, breaking into pieces—mirroring the way I was feeling broken apart.

"What do you mean you're moving?" I demanded. "What about me and Josh?"

Her answer was so bizarre that it left me speechless.

"Well . . . you can come if you want," she said flatly.

What was she thinking? Springfield, Illinois, was three hours away. She was planning to just up and leave her sixteen-year-old and thirteen-year-old on their own? The answer was plain. *Yes. That is what she wanted.* But I knew what I wanted as well.

"I have one year of high school left. I'm *not* going anywhere."

I was incensed. For the past three years, I'd felt that Josh and I had been on our own anyway. She had been absent from our lives and preoccupied with her succession of men. But now, before my senior year? And with Josh just finishing seventh grade? Was she honestly going to leave us and move three hours away? Yes.

And just like that, she did.

We were literally on our own. No parent. Just the two kids.

Dad instantly scrambled to move from the Chicago area to nearby St. Charles, a half hour from Burlington, so that we could live with him. Poor Josh had to switch to a different school. I managed to stay at my high school in Burlington by driving myself thirty minutes each way.

The fighter would do whatever needed to be done. So what if I were a failure? So what if I wasn't good enough? So what if I was alone and abandoned? I was nobody's victim. I would control my own life.

Chapter 6

FILLING HOLES

"People are slaves to whatever has mastered them."
2 PETER 2:19

"Can you come with me, please?" The voice—deep, male, full of authority—spoke when Mom and I had barely stepped out of the mall entrance of Kohl's. I thought the loud pounding of my heart was going to give me away. But it didn't. The security guard didn't need my telltale heart; he already knew I was trying to walk out with merchandise I hadn't paid for.

Mom had driven from Springfield to visit Josh and me for the weekend and had offered to take me shopping—an attempt at a mom-and-daughter activity. While in Kohl's, I went to the dressing room, telling Mom I was going to try on two or three bras and some underwear—$52 worth of clothing. Then I put my clothes on over them and walked out. It certainly wasn't the only time I shoplifted; it was just the only time I got caught. But what had possessed me to do it while I was out with my mom? Mom had the money and could have paid for it. Did I think they'd be less likely to suspect me? Did I do it that day out of habit? Or out of a need to feel that adrenaline rush of power, especially since I'd be outwitting not only the store but Mom as well? Or out of anger in a lame attempt to punish Mom for leaving us? Her abrupt departure had torn a jagged black hole in me, one that I could not stitch together and find a way to heal. Instead, I had started to fall into that hole.

At the security guard's first words, Mom looked at him, baffled. Then she looked at me, and she could easily tell by the look on my face that the guard knew something she didn't. She followed us back to the security office and sat quietly with me as the police were called. I was told to step into a separate room and remove the stolen items. I complied. Then we looked at the "evidence" on the security guard's desk. How ironic that I chose underwear. It represented what Mom had never even talked to me about—becoming a woman, what body changes to expect during puberty. Sexuality. She had left me on my own on all fronts.

I felt mostly numb as I was arrested and handcuffed. After finger-printing me and filing charges, they released me on my own recognizance, with the not-so-pleasant farewell words, "We'll see you in court."

I'm not sure what I expected Mom's reaction to be. Anger? Embarrass-ment? To my surprise, she expressed neither. Maybe she somehow sensed my anger at her for abandoning Josh and me. Did she feel guilty, even responsible, for my acting out? I didn't know, and frankly, I didn't much care.

Mom and Dad both came to court with me and sat in silent support as I confessed, taking full responsibility. I left court with a misdemeanor on my record. (Thankfully, a few years later, my record was cleared because I hadn't done it again.)

As I look back, it seems so weird that I stole at all—not just that day, but all the other shoplifting days too. It's not like I needed to. After all, I'd had jobs since I was thirteen. I wanted to carry my own weight. Make my own way. Earn my own money for my own expenses.

I did it not because I needed to; I did it to fill a hole.

THE QUEST FOR CONTROL

Looking in from the outside, my senior year seemed to be filled with laughing, enjoying friends, and getting ready for the send-off into adult-hood. I may have acted as though I had it together, but on the inside, I was dying. Even though my mother had not been a nurturing presence in my adolescent years, she was still my mother, and she had many wonderful qualities. I couldn't control her horrific personal crisis or her unusual ways of dealing with life, kids, and household responsibilities. But I loved her and needed her, and her abrupt departure had torn a jagged black hole in me, one that I could not stitch together, one that would not heal.

It seemed that though Mom came to a few of my games that year, she was there in body but gone in spirit. The picture of my life with her in it was fading, dissolving, like the picture Marty McFly was holding in *Back to the Future* when it appeared that his parents would never meet.

The substitutes I found for my broken identity and fragile self-image, an intact family, and my mother's love were unhealthy and unhelpful. Fast food. Drugs. Alcohol. Shoplifting. Sexual activity.

It also explains something else: my anorexia.

Anorexia is an eating disorder characterized by an obsession with weight loss, looking thin, and either refusing to eat or obsessively controlling what one eats. According to ANAD (the National Association of Anorexia Nervosa and Associated Disorders), at least thirty million people of all ages and genders suffer from this eating disorder in the United States.* But I didn't set out to be anorexic. I had been a Taco-Bell-eating, volleyball-playing, sports-loving jock. As an athlete and teenager, I naturally burned plenty of calories daily and still managed be in the normal weight range. Anorexia crept into my life insidiously.

It probably got a jump start when I moved to St. Charles, Illinois, with my dad and found a job at a health club, where I worked nights and weekends scrubbing toilets and showers and working the front desk. There I was exposed for the first time to the vanity so prevalent in the fitness and gym culture. Not the normal vanity we all have to some degree, but that of many who seemed compelled to do vigorous daily workouts.

---

* "Eating Disorder Statistics," *ANAD*, www.anad.org/get-information/about-eating-disorders/eating-disorders-statistics (accessed February 22, 2017).

It fascinated me that everywhere I looked at the club, I saw powerful, beautiful people. Smiling. Glowing. *Perfect.*

I began by adding more workouts to my sports activities. I started counting every calorie. I put myself on a strict fat-free diet, eating rice cakes, grapes, fat-free crackers, popcorn, and frozen yogurt. I wanted to be a perfect version of me—skinnier, smarter, prettier. I started out my senior year weighing 122 pounds. I found pleasure and strength in the process of losing weight. But even more, I found the very thing I was desperate to have: *control.*

Could I control the choices my mother made? No. Could I control the things she did that embarrassed me? No. Could I control the labels others had put on me and my family? No. Or the labels I'd put on myself? I didn't think so. But I could control what I put into my mouth. How much. How many calories. How many fat grams. That steadied me. It gave me a sense of order in my extremely disordered world—which led me to focus on food more and more.

The painful darkness that had been growing from my earliest childhood through my teen years was gnawing away at my spirit. I tried desperately to find something to make it go away. It's funny that though my mother's behavior brought me great shame and embarrassment, my own choices and my own behavior in going along with my friends brought me no shame at all. *Everybody* slept with their boyfriend. *Everybody* smoked or drank or experimented with acid. *Everybody* shoplifted. These were just cool things to do. There was no sense of making a moral choice, no sense of guilt, of doing something wrong. So I kept on doing all the things everyone else did, waiting for the moment when my inner pain vanished—just as my mother had vanished.

Not that all my high school behavior was unhealthy. I always held a job, played sports year-round, and got good grades. I never got in "trouble" in high school. I appeared to have it together, and my reputation with teachers and other grown-ups was good. I wasn't loud, partying, obnoxious, or trouble seeking. In fact, I had lots of friends, and though I was still shy and reserved, I totally enjoyed the laughter, camaraderie, and just plain goofiness of teenagers having a good time. Being a people pleaser was vitally important to me, and so I enjoyed being friendly, funny, silly, and welcomed (quietly) into a room by teachers as well as classmates. But all of that was a mask to the internal devastation I privately worked so hard to control.

I lost a pound. And then another. By graduation, I had lost twenty-two pounds. For an athletically built girl who was five foot five and 122 pounds to begin with, twenty-two pounds was a significant amount of weight. I wouldn't have admitted it then, even to myself, but this was my acceptable, nearly invisible, slow suicide.

It took its toll. I didn't have the energy or the drive to think about the future. Coping with my confusing life zapped all my energy. Froze my thought processes. While other kids were eagerly making plans, signing up for college, and marching forward into their futures, I was stuck in the private black hole that had become my life, clawing at the dirt, choking on the dust. The Bible reads, "Where there is no vision, the people perish" (Proverbs 29:18 KJV). I had no vision. I was seriously depressed. I had no idea what I wanted to do with my life. I couldn't see any further into my future than losing the next pound. My only goal was to lose more weight.

Unlike my more forward-thinking, motivated classmates, I had no idea what to do after graduation, especially knowing I'd have to pay my own way through college and not wanting to go into debt. At the last minute, figuring I had to do something, I signed up at Elgin Community College to take some basic courses.

SLOW SUICIDE

A few weeks after graduation, our group of friends and classmates took a trip to Puerto Vallarta. Everyone was a bit crazy with the excitement of our first taste of our newfound freedom. We would be able to drink legally in Mexico (and boy, did we!). But while everyone else was gorging on Mexican food, I was eating the food I'd packed and brought with me—crackers and microwave SpaghettiOs. I sampled only a little bit of local foods. Despite that, I returned home very sick, most likely from a parasite I picked up there. This trip was something I had looked forward to for a long time. But it, too, disappointed.

Even so, I told myself that at least something good had come of my trip to Mexico: I lost another three pounds that month, bringing me down to ninety-seven pounds.

As the pounds fell away, friends and family noticed and urged me to eat. But I resented their interference. As I saw it, it was my body, my decision, my way. By this time, I had lost control over my anorexia. Because of the parasite, I totally lost my appetite and was in far too deep.

Mom came back for a brief visit. At dinner, I could tell she was watching me portion out my food. She said, "You're too thin, and you're not eating enough."

"I'm fine, Mom."

Deeply concerned, she called a doctor anyway. The moment the doctor entered the exam room, Mom said, "There's something wrong here. I think my daughter is anorexic." For once I felt seen by her, even though I was disappearing. She'd noticed *something*.

The doctor put his stethoscope to my chest and said, "Well, she *is* thin." He peered into my ears with his little light, up my nostrils, and down my throat. After examining me, the doctor gave Mom a prescription that was supposed to help me. Mom had done what she could, but I didn't respond well to the drugs. One of them caused hallucinations. I stopped taking them a few weeks later but never told Mom.

It became more and more difficult for me to go to work at the fitness club. I could barely get out of bed, much less perform the tasks required of me. Then one day, I got to work, and the doors of the fitness club had been chained shut. They had not been paying the rent, so the landlord locked them out. With a good deal of relief, I went home and crawled back into bed.

Later that summer, still living with my dad in St. Charles, I went to the grocery store and ran into my high school best friend. Instead of saying hello, she just looked at me, with her mouth open in astonishment. I can't blame her. I was a walking skeleton. My legs were like pencil sticks. My skinny arms were covered with a sweatshirt despite the summer heat. I was cold—always cold. I barely had the energy to shower and brush my teeth, so I certainly didn't have the energy to carry on even a casual conversation. I had nothing left to give anyone. I said hello and made awkward small talk. Today I regret that I was too self-conscious to tell her how much her friendship meant to me. I haven't seen her since.

Soon I was down to a mere seventy-eight pounds. I knew I was sick, but I was clueless about the damage I was doing to myself in my pursuit of losing just one more pound. I didn't know I was knocking on death's door. Electrolyte imbalance could have stopped my heart. I should have been hospitalized, but I had turned eighteen in July and our insurance wouldn't cover in-patient hospitalization, even though I was still under my parents' policy. An eating disorder was considered a psychiatric disorder, and the cost of a month of in-patient treatment was more than $100,000. There was no way my parents could ever come up with that much money.

So I went to two weeks of outpatient treatment instead. There they tried to stuff me with piles of meat and potatoes, cookies and cake. I was horrified, literally afraid of what I now considered disgusting Midwestern fare. I was angry, and the entire experience just made me feel even sicker.

And then Dad came home one day with an announcement that surprised and delighted me.

HOPE

"I've received a job transfer to San Diego," Dad said. He invited Josh and me to move with him. I was exhilarated and began anticipating a new beginning. A fresh start. A blank slate.

On Halloween, Dad took me to the airport and put me on a plane. He and Josh would follow with the dog and the car, driving from Illinois to California. I didn't want to drive all that way with them—besides, our dog, Jake, already made me sneeze. Being shut in a car for days with it seemed an intolerable idea.

The three of us stayed in an apartment for three months until Dad found the right house. I was grateful when my older brother, Jason, moved from Arizona to live with us as well. Finally, with the three of us and Dad together, maybe we would feel like a family again. But sadly, by now I'd developed a snarky attitude. With an air of entitlement, I pointed out that my furniture was bigger than everyone else's, and as I was the only girl, I needed the biggest bedroom with a private bathroom—the master bedroom. My dad didn't even hesitate to give it to me. I felt he owed me. *After all*, I reasoned, *he had left us with a dysfunctional mother.* Dad carried a load of guilt, believing that he *did* owe me. Usually I didn't take advantage of that guilt, because I prided myself on being self-sufficient. But this time I didn't care.

Once we were settled into our new home in sunny California, I felt something I hadn't felt in a long time: hope. A new beginning! I took walks on the beach, alone and with my dad. I enjoyed my brothers. I wanted to get started on my new life, and I got a job at Islands, a burger restaurant. But I had to quit after only a couple weeks because I lacked the stamina to do my job of bussing tables. I went home and back to bed.

Here, languishing in bed rather than enjoying my new life in sunny California, the familiar voices were back in my head: Despite the hope I felt on arriving in a perpetually sunny, beautiful place, I had brought along issues that didn't magically dissolve. The shadows had grown too dark for me to simply walk out of them. The hole too dank. The pain too overwhelming. The lies too powerful.

For the next six months, I was almost too weak to get out of bed, barely able to shower. Getting out of bed took so much energy that I just stayed there, stuck in my dark hole. On those days, I wondered if there was light somewhere. I knew there must be. But where? And how could I find it if I never clawed my way out?

Oddly enough (and very true of eating disorders), I was obsessed with food. Instead of eating, I lay in bed endlessly watching the Food Network on my nineteen-inch TV. On the very few times I did venture out of the house, I went to the grocery store. Food was the only thing I could control, and yet I was starving.

People who have never suffered from or studied anorexia wonder how someone could do such harm to his or her body. Why can't they just look in the mirror and see how skinny they are, and then eat something? But that's not how it works—if it were that easy, no one would be anorexic. When I looked in the mirror, I didn't see a skeleton in the mirror; I still saw a fat person. Doctors have a name for that—body dysmorphic disorder—and it can spring from unresolved feelings and trauma. I refused to gain weight.

Dad couldn't understand that anorexia is a disease of the mind. It made him angry and frustrated. He'd come home from work and urge me to join him and my brothers for dinner. I'd refuse to get out of bed. "Eat some food!" he would finally bellow. "What are you doing to yourself? Andrea, you've got to eat!"

Then he tried to get me to drink some nutrition shakes. The shakes were awful, and after drinking a few, I started to gain weight—so I guess they were doing their job. But they were filled with sugar and fat, and when I consumed them, all I could see was all that processed junk going into my body.

One night I refused to drink any more of them.

"I'm eighteen. I'm an adult," I screamed. "Nobody can force me into eating." I was right, and Dad knew it, which undoubtedly made him feel powerless to help me. And that powerlessness enraged him.

My dad is pretty mellow and laid-back. And I had only seen him lose his temper a couple times in my life. But that night, the father who had never been violent with me became furious, because he was so afraid of me dying. I could see the fear in his eyes when he lost it. He took hold of my legs and swiped them off the bed, while I stubbornly screamed my refusal.

My older brother stepped in, and they began to fight. Jason and Dad got into it, while I sat on the floor crying, watching my brother step up to protect me for the first time in his life. My big brother. The one who, while we were growing up, used to say, "You're ugly, Brace Face. Those glasses make you look stupid." But that night, he stepped up. And when my dad had cooled and backed off, Jason looked at me, pleading. "Please, please, Andrea. You've got to drink this stuff. Or eat. Something." Tears rolled down his face. I will never forget that day that my big brother truly cared for me and tried to help. From that moment on, our relationship changed. He was, is today, and will always be my sweet big brother.

And so I took a can and drank it. And I never touched another one again.

I was so stubborn. I would not relinquish the control I believed anorexia had given me. But I was blind to the fact that I was *not* in control. How could I not see that it was anorexia that had control over me?

ON OUR OWN AGAIN

Around that time, Dad met a woman, Pat, through work, He quickly began to spend much of his time with her and very little with us, until he was primarily living with her more than in our home. The old, familiar sense of emotional abandonment pounded away at my heart. I tried to slam my emotional door shut on the feelings that were far too familiar. Was this a pattern in my family? Would everyone who was supposed to love me abandon me for someone better?

Meanwhile, Jason found a bank job and started going to school. He too found a girlfriend. So once again, Josh and I were on our own, with no parental guidance, no time together as a family—at all. Food had been my primary substitute for feeling a sense of belonging and love since my elementary school days. Now I watched as my little brother dealt with his pain and absence of parental attention by smoking pot and getting into trouble. Dad put him in a transitional high school, hoping that would help him. But what Josh needed was his family—not a different school. He was hanging on by a thread.

At three o'clock one morning, I got a phone call. "Andrea," Josh said, mumbling, "you've gotta come get me."

"What? Where are you?"

"Jail."

My heart sunk. "What happened?" I said softly, not wanting to wake my other brother.

"I was just goofing off with some friends."

"Doing what?" I didn't know if I should be angry or heartsick that he was so lost.

"Spray-painting. It's no big deal. I do it all the time."

I sighed as I hung up the phone, but I knew I'd do anything for him. I made my way to the police station as quickly as I could to bring him home, all the while with memories in my mind of playing the role of mom for Josh in my elementary, junior high, and high school days. I'd been there for him as well as I'd been able. He was my buddy. He still needed me, and I didn't want to abandon him.

But I didn't want to abandon myself either. Everyone else had chosen other priorities over family. I was tempted, especially because I was so weak, to play the victim and simply let myself waste away to nothing. But that very idea triggered the old fighter in me to rise up. I wasn't going to let all of their choices define me! I had come to San Diego for a new start—and it was time to start.

I made a conscious decision to increase my food intake. I started eating more fruits, vegetables, protein, and even more fun food, including sugar and fat. I also started dating a sweet guy, a surfer who often liked to go out to eat. I didn't want to expose my anorexia, so I ate with him. And I no longer wanted to be too weak and lethargic to get out of bed. When I grew strong enough, I got a job at a clothing store in the mall. And with that income, I decided to start classes at the community college that January.

A GOAL AT LAST

Walking into a community college in a new city, I found myself feeling I could begin a brand-new life with a clean slate. I didn't know a soul there. When in my fourth month of living in California I showed up to register for classes, I had no idea what to take—but I noticed a theatre class that still had openings. I put it on my list. I'd had no interest in theatre or drama in high school. I was always too shy, too self-conscious. Besides, I was an athlete, not an actor, and in my high school those two worlds didn't mix. In my circle, acting hadn't been the cool thing to do.

I quickly discovered that theatre class was an invigorating place to make new friends and create a new identity for myself. By nature, I am an introvert, so I had always bottled up my pain, my feelings, and my voice. But once I started theatre and began playing someone else, creating characters, I felt a sense of incredible release. It was cathartic. Plus, I got to escape being me and thinking about all of my problems. I felt free.

Physically, I gradually got better. Not cured, not "over it"—but better than before. I don't know if it was because of my sense of responsibility for Josh, or because I finally hated feeling sick or weak, or because I wanted to earn money. Probably a combination of all three. But I knew for sure that part of the reason was that I wanted to get to theatre class for every single session. I didn't want to miss anything. I wanted to have the energy to act. I'd actually found something that sparked my imagination and drive—something other than simply my failed quest for control.

Slowly, I began to trade anorexia for the freedom of this new life. I realized that here in California, I could be whomever I wanted to be. Nobody knew my mother and her embarrassing choices or my family issues. Nobody knew my junk. I found myself in an entirely new place. And it was a great place to be.

In acting class, I first experienced the marvel of stepping into another character—and there I found tremendous freedom, unlike any I'd ever known before. It was an escape from my own pain and baggage and an inviting opportunity to take on and experiment with whole new personas I *could* become should I choose. I found great freedom in escaping "me" and my issues and problems and diving into someone else. I was meeting a new self in a way I had never imagined, and to my complete shock, I *liked* who I met there.

"Dad, I've decided I'm going to become an actor," I announced enthusiastically one day.

My father tried to "talk some sense" into me. Some laughed at the mere mention of my becoming an actor. My coworkers told me story after story of acting wannabes working retail, serving at restaurants, working hotel jobs, and doing pretty much anything other than finding paying work in acting. "Good luck with that!" and "Yeah, you and everyone else come to California to be an actor" pretty much summed up everyone's response to my newfound passion.

My self-doubts surfaced again for a brief time. Could I *really* become an actor? It seemed crazy. But something inside me came alive when I acted. I was liberated, and I felt like I was discovering who I was as I explored the thoughts and feelings of other characters. Though I had never been in the spotlight in front of people, had never shined brightly at anything, and had felt self-conscious and unworthy all my life, those very thoughts drove the fighter in me even more. Impossible odds? Unlikely success? Acting made me feel something I'd never felt before. Why *couldn't* I become an actor?

And then I made a decision. I'd prove them all wrong.

I did some research and signed first with the Nouveau Model & Talent agency in La Jolla. My agent set me up for headshots, and I was auditioning soon thereafter. That sounded encouraging. Through Nouveau, I started picking up some modeling work in San Diego.

Nouveau then referred me to a Hollywood agent, Gary, who, as they explained it, would help me achieve my goals. Within a few days, I was heading north from San Diego in my little red Honda Civic to meet Gary. My palms were sweaty with nervousness when I shook hands with him, but I tapped into my newfound acting skills to act confident and self-assured. "You need some more photos for your comp card," Gary told me. "I'll set you up with a guy who photographs a lot of Playmates." "Huh? Um, okay . . ." I blindly fell into this sham.

Show business is full of predators, and as it turned out, it didn't take me long to figure out that this recommended photographer was one. I shudder to think of how many wide-eyed and innocent young girls have been mistreated and preyed on by him at their time of greatest vulnerability. But then when he said, "Would you like to go to a party at Hugh Hefner's Playboy Mansion? There's no better place to network than at Hef's," I had an answer.

"Um . . . Sure!"

I couldn't wait.

Chapter 7

A MANSION WITH MANY ROOMS

The path of the righteous is like the morning sun,
shining ever brighter till the full light of day.
But the way of the wicked is like deep darkness;
they do not know what makes them stumble.
PROVERBS 4:18–19

I tapped the steering wheel to the music blaring from my radio as I pointed my Honda Civic north on I-5 from San Diego in the fading light of dusk. The Playboy Mansion. The *Playboy Mansion*! It's not as if going to the mansion was ever on the list of things I wanted to do—or ever thought I would do. But now that I had an actual invitation and a promise from the photographer who had arranged for the invitation that I would meet all sorts of celebrities, how could I *not* go? Would I meet people in the business who might help me reach my dream, or at least point me in the right direction? The acting bug had bitten, giving me an insatiable desire to perform. Maybe this was the chance of a lifetime. Besides, parties at the mansion were the stuff of Hollywood legend. Who threw better parties than Hugh Hefner?

I turned my radio up, hoping the sound would drown out my racing thoughts so that I could focus on the drive. Destination: Holmby Hills, a small elite neighborhood tucked between Beverly Hills and Westwood. Aaron Spelling's mansion was just five houses down the narrow street from the Playboy Mansion, so this was a very ritzy area.

Two and a half hours later, at dusk, I exited the 405 onto Wilshire Boulevard. My directions instructed me to turn left up the hill after the UCLA campus. Another turn, and I found myself on a narrow street lined with high walls of thick vegetation, like a walled road through a secret garden. A sharp left, and there it was, on my right. I don't know what I was expecting—something stately and awe-inspiring, I suppose—but the property's smallish, ornate, wrought iron gates were not it. As I turned into the drive, there was a small boulder on my left that I'd been told to watch for. I rolled down my window, stuck my head out, and—feeling a strange mixture of foolishness and privilege—spoke to the rock. "Hi, I'm on the list for your party." At least I *hoped* the commercial agent had followed through and put me on the list.

The gates slowly swung open. I put my Honda into gear and followed the driveway up the hill. Then to my left I saw it: the mansion. Gothic-Tudor style, set like a magical castle nestled in a thick forest. The fountain in front burbled, its water highlighted by blue lights. Banks of colored lights illuminated the grounds of the nearly 22,000-square-foot mansion. From the roof, a winged gargoyle glared down at the guests' cars below like an overgrown bat. Talk about drama! This place was built to impress. Rolls Royces and Bentleys, Ferraris and Maseratis, parked neatly next to each other. My little Honda Civic certainly didn't belong. Did *I*?

Headlights behind me flickered, so I moved on up the driveway, the mansion disappearing from sight until I rounded another curve. There stood fifteen beautiful men in tuxes lined up along the curved, stone driveway.

One of the tuxedoed gentlemen waved me to a stop, opened my door, and reached out a hand. "Welcome, Miss." I put my hand in his with an involuntary shiver. He gestured toward a stone archway that led to the grounds, so I moved in that direction with all the elegance I could muster, hoping not to trip and make a fool of myself. I felt a little embarrassed showing up alone. But I also felt as if I could do this—as if I were an actor playing the role of "new actor finding her way in the acting world."

◦ ✤ ◦

I stood before the archway for just a moment, wondering what I would discover on the other side. Then I slipped through and stopped, frozen.

I had stepped into a magical garden of glamour and sensuality such as I had never dreamed of. Everywhere I looked there were beautiful people, their diamonds flashing in the colorful lights that gently illuminated the back garden. All around me glided beautiful women dressed in designer dresses that clung to every curve. Some exposed as much skin as possible without revealing absolutely everything. Others did reveal everything— covering themselves only in body paint. And the breasts! Oh my. Fake breasts, bare breasts, breasts everywhere.

And here I was, in my comparatively modest $18 black dress from Forever 21—the one I had thought was cute. And in that dress, my own original B-cup breasts, delivered not by a plastic surgeon but naturally.

Playboy bunnies in pink and black bunny suits moved through the crowd, some carrying a tray of drinks or appetizers, but most simply just skimming by guests, chatting to some, laughing with others, posing for photos—alone and with guests.

A man tipped back his head and laughed contagiously. When I turned to him, I had to consciously close my jaw, which had just dropped. George Clooney stood within feet of me, and wow, was he stunning! Even the men were pretty!

Moments later, Leonardo DiCaprio walked by, flanked by two bunnies, looking even more handsome, if possible, than he did in *Titanic*.

Doing my best not to stare, I turned aside and walked toward the famous pool and grotto, its clear water lit from underneath. Throughout the garden, soft, hidden lights made the bushes and trees gently glow.

What was I doing here?

It took me a little while to find my agent, Gary. I thanked him for arranging for my invitation, and we chatted briefly. When he wandered away, I played it chill, as always, and kept my insecurities to myself—but that didn't mean they weren't surging through me. I had clearly entered a different world. And I was alone.

I wandered over to the fountain, admiring it, wondering what I was supposed to do next—trying to look cool but feeling overwhelmed. I had simply never guessed how large this party would be.

"Hi," said a silky, feminine voice. Someone was suddenly standing next to me. I looked to my side and saw an incredibly beautiful blonde woman, about five foot seven, with striking blue eyes and a perfect figure. She had all the poise and confidence I lacked and longed for. "I'm Sarah. You're new, aren't you?"

I nodded, trying on a smile. "First time. Is it that obvious?" I didn't sense any condescension from her despite my off-the-rack dress and black heels from the discount store in the mall.

"Come on. Let's get you a drink, and I'll introduce you around."

Surprised, I nearly said, "Who—me?" I was a nobody. Why such hospitality? But I soon discovered how friendly most of the people were. As Sarah and I made the rounds, I felt surprisingly welcomed. By the time I met the infamous Hef, I felt almost at home, ready to give an honest smile and leave all the butterflies behind. Hef looked into my eyes, smiled, and lifted my hand and did something no man had ever done before—he placed a gentle kiss on the back of it. "It's always nice to meet a friend of Sarah's." It was sweet and unexpected. I liked him immediately.

I fell into an easy pace with Sarah. Her sweetness and genuine nature drew me in as she guided me through a grand tour of the gardens, the exotic animal zoo, and portions of the mansion. I couldn't shake the feeling that I'd stepped from reality onto the silver screen itself and become a part of the magic of the movies.

Somehow, a few hours flew by quickly, so with the two-hour-plus drive ahead of me, I decided I'd better head back to my dad's place in San Diego. Before I left, at Sarah's request, I wrote down my phone number and address, thinking she was probably just asking to be nice. But a few days later, she called to say hi—and to invite me to the next party. I later discovered that Sarah was one of Hef's three main girlfriends.

A Hugh Hefner party wasn't so much one party as it was a collection of parties throughout the mansion and grounds. Each room housed a different activity—an orgy in one, a card game in another, and people hooking up everywhere. Freedom reigned. Drinking, drugs, sex, gambling—you name it, it was there for the taking. All those separate parties made it easy for me to stay as "clean" as I wanted, so I just avoided those rooms and kept to the pool and central gathering areas.

There was never any pressure on me to give or do more than I wanted, no hint of judgment for anything one did or didn't do, and I appreciated that. I had never felt so accepted and unjudged in my life, and given my history, my yearning to belong, it felt wonderful to show up and simply be free to be myself—inexpensive little black dress, small breasts, and mall shoes included.

The mansion drew me back like a magnet time and time again. I felt honored to be invited to the parties, and before long, I was up there every weekend, often (at Sarah's invitation) spending the night (alone) in one of the twelve bedrooms, which saved me the long drive back to San Diego late at night. Many young actors looking for a break would have clawed their way to get an invitation to these parties. Unless you received a personal invitation and got your name placed on the guest list, the only way to be considered for entrance was to send a headshot and résumé and wait for an approval, which more often than not was declined. So I treasured my time there, never quite sure how my agent had secured my name on the list.

Famous industry people were part of the fabric of these parties. I met many movie stars—Rod Stewart, Colin Farrell, Leonardo DiCaprio along with his crew, and the Hollywood list goes on and on. Hundreds of past and current Playmates, which equaled a whole lot of perfect people—or so I thought. Pamela Anderson, in particular, was so sweet. When Sarah introduced me to her one evening, I blurted out, "Oh my gosh, you are so beautiful!" And I truly meant it.

She gave me a genuine smile and said warmly, "Sweetheart, so are you." I'll never forget that. Most celebrities are too into themselves to see beyond their own mirror. They would answer, "Oh, thank you," and then move on as though you don't matter. But not Pamela.

Hef loved get-togethers. He genuinely seemed to enjoy people, and I watched how effortlessly he interacted with people. In my experience, he was a very kindhearted man who watched out for me. At dinner, as he made the rounds of the tables and greeted each guest, he would bend down to me to say quietly, "Make sure you eat." One time he added, "If you want to pose for *Playboy*, you've got to gain weight." I never saw the sexual side of him, perhaps because it was clear that I wouldn't welcome that.

It's so obvious to me, looking back, the risks and dangers I was exposing myself to at these parties and how skewed my perceptions were of the people and the culture. But I had nothing in my life up to that point that would have prepared me to exercise better judgment about that world.

On the one hand, it's as if I had no moral compass at all, so I easily adjusted to cocktail conversation in a circle where one person might be topless, one garbed in a stunning tuxedo, and another in a see-through dress—as if sexual freedom and self-expression were the highest of values.

And yet, on the other hand, I instinctively avoided invitations to some rooms, recoiling at the thought of what was happening behind those doors. Oh, how differently I see that experience today than I did at the naive age of nineteen. In fact, I find it amazing—and eye-opening—that even without my conscious awareness of any reasons behind my instincts, there was a True North drawing me toward more wholesome choices and steering me clear of the slippery slope downward.

Today, I know a truth that eluded me at the time: God has graciously given us a conscience and an instinctive knowledge of himself and his rules for life. My own internal moral compass may have been broken, but True North beckoned me nonetheless! Much of what was going on around me at the mansion, especially in some of the rooms I always avoided, was a violation of how God designed us to behave, to treat ourselves and others. And there were other things occurring that I didn't think were necessarily wrong; they just weren't for me. I was numb to sin on some levels, and on other levels clearly sensitive to it. With repeated visits, much of what at first seemed wrong came to seem normal. After a while, we become numb to what is wrong and reach for those behaviors that violate our Designer's intentions. A passage in Romans explains:

> Therefore God gave them over in the sinful desires of their hearts to sexual impurity for the degrading of their bodies with one another. They exchanged the truth about God for a lie, and worshiped and served created things rather than the Creator—who is forever praised. Because of this, God gave them over to shameful lusts.
>
> ROMANS 1:24–26

What I didn't know then is that once you have the Holy Spirit guiding you, the more you pray and seek him, the more sin bothers you. Back then, I would have never believed what I would soon be willing to do for a paycheck and an opportunity to be "discovered." For, as Hef's comment at dinner that night illustrated, now I was seen as in the Playboy stable, considered a possible model for *Playboy*. Oh, how God protected me!

A MIDSUMMER NIGHT'S DREAM

Within a few weeks, Sarah said, "Do you want to rent a place together? I found a house in North Hollywood, and my friend Olivia and I need a roommate."

The moment she asked, I was ready to go. Then my responsible side kicked in, and I hesitated. "What would I do for work?" I asked. I'd have to give up my job waiting tables at a restaurant in San Diego, making minimum wage plus tips. If I had to settle for the same type of job in Los Angeles, I wasn't sure I could make ends meet.

Sarah waved a hand dismissively. "That's easy. I'll hook you up when you get here."

So on July 30, I left San Diego for good. I had to leave behind the red Honda, since it was my dad's, so I bought a cute little teal Isuzu and packed it up, along with a U-Haul. I'd been casually dating a sweet guy, a surfer, for almost a year, and he offered to drive it for me, even though I'd just broken up with him. Off I went, with $350 left in my bank account.

My portion of the shared rent for that little house in North Hollywood was $630. It was a nice house, but nothing special. I didn't care! It was my first real step away from my family toward independence, and I was excited.

Soon after I moved in with Sarah and Olivia came *the* event of the year at the Playboy Mansion—the Midsummer Night's Dream party. The party required attendees to wear lingerie. Not a big deal for a guy—they can always arrive and then just strip down to a pair of silk boxers or pajamas in the style Hef was famous for. Women's attire, on the other hand, required much forethought. The lingerie needn't be any more risqué than a bikini, but somehow, no matter the style, it *all* felt risqué. The women, including me, drove there already outfitted in our "costumes"—no fair changing into it after you got there. There were see-through teddies, tap pants and camisoles, corsets and hose with garter belts, and women looking as though they were models for the most sensuous lingerie stores imaginable. One scantily dressed woman, nearly nude, sat on a rock in the middle of the pool, reciting lines from Shakespeare's *Midsummer Night's Dream*. There was something beautiful and very erotic about all these people dressed for bed—and I don't mean climbing into bed to sleep.

Afterward, I went on and on about the party to my mother, and she was so impressed that she insisted on coming the following year. How many women would even consider going to such a party accompanied by their mother? I may be the only one.

At the party the next summer, Mom didn't seem remotely self-conscious about parading about in her white lingerie. Strange as it may sound—and yes, it is strange—the party seemed to bring us temporarily closer. It was I, her Hollywood daughter, who introduced her to the infamous Hef, the man who, for Mom's generation, defined sexuality, the breaking of social mores, and the mainstreaming of what had previously been a hidden, disreputable industry. Mom saw the party as very glamorous, just as I did—certainly as the world defines glamour.

MY FIRST STAGE

Sarah was true to her word. The Monday following my first Midsummer Night's Dream party, she had a job idea for me. "I got you an interview at a bikini bar. You've got the body for it."

"What?" I asked. "What's a bikini bar?"

"Well, it's like you're a stripper, but you only strip down to your bikini and dance to music on stage."

I stared at her. "I can't do that."

"Look," she reassured me, "think of it like being a dancer. There's no full nudity. Just a few topless nights every now and then. It's a celebration of your body! It can be really fun. And you can make a *lot* of money. That's how I started off."

I thought of my reaction to my mother's lifestyle choices during my teens and her need for attention from men. She lived as if her motto was, "Do your own thing. Don't worry about what other people think or say." I squirmed at the memory of being thirteen and fourteen and feeling like I was more mature than she was—that I had to mother my mother because she had embarrassed me so. I'd had to grow up so fast. Was I really willing now to walk away from the values that had come naturally to me in those days?

But by now, I had slipped into rationalizing that moral code away, dismissing it as childish, restrictive, unsophisticated. Here in Hollywood, I was spending most of my time around twenty-five- to forty-five-year-olds who lived the life I was trying to adopt as my own. I was beginning to accomplish my dream, hanging around all the money, the fame, and the best-looking people on the planet. I was making it, or so I thought. I looked up to them. They were confident, secure, successful, and beautiful. With role models like those, my moral compass didn't raise much objection to my working as a dancer in a bikini bar. Not much nudity? Wear a bathing suit? Hey, it must not be too bad. And the money I could make for just dancing was amazing. I wasn't excited about it, but I needed a job. So I made a choice: I would simply follow Sarah's lead—so worldly and wise at twenty-five. I would focus on the "fun" and "good money" part of the job. After all, I had a new life in a new place with new friends. Why not a new kind of work as well? I took the job at the bikini bar.

Was I scared? Terrified. After all, I was shy, had always been a modest dresser, and had struggled with my self-image since childhood.

The bar was in Pasadena, a small, respectable place—if you can call any bikini bar respectable. The building was in a well-lit, seemingly safe area, but it always felt creepy to me. On my first day, my stomach clenched as soon as I walked in. I felt so dirty, so compromised. *What have I come to?* I wondered.

And yet I stayed. I felt as though I didn't have a lot of options and should give this a try. I could give it at least one shift.

The inside was a typical dark bar, with smoke and mirrors and men. Lots of men, of course. Goes with the territory. Most of the interior was bathed in low light, and mirrors lined the back of the stage. I and the other dancers would emerge onto the raised stage from behind a curtain and take our positions. Chairs lined the front edge of the stage so that the patrons could be close to any dancer who chose to perform near the edge.

We were encouraged to choose our own stage names and personas, and I selected "Sunny" as mine. We could be flamboyant and interactive with the clientele, or we could keep our distance. I always danced as far from a client's groping touches as I could, but many dancers chose spots near the edge, where they knew they'd earn much higher tips. My first night, as I danced in the smoke-filled air beneath the spotlights, I was horrified and felt like I'd stepped into a nightmare. I made it a point to never watch myself in a mirror, as I knew I would have hated to see the woman looking back at me.

Yet I returned the next night and the next. My sense of disgust never faded, but somehow my sense of horror over the behavior unfolding before me (and *by* me) diminished over time into a sad realization that lust, loneliness, and desperation made for an ugly, empty combination. If the desire for true intimacy is what drove anyone into that place, I knew they'd never find it there. And though many of my coworkers would pretend to be aroused by or impressed with the men there, backstage we all understood that our clients were barely tolerable. It was all show. It was theatre. I was on stage, but this was far from the kind of acting I wanted to do.

I didn't dance as much as I simply moved with the music, but men seemed to respond to me—and so to please them, I did things I'm not proud of. I cringe today at the memories. A few times, picking up some extra work in another bar at the encouragement of one of my girlfriends,

I even took my top off. I hated that I did that. I felt pressured and didn't have the boldness to say no. I felt angry, but I didn't know if I was angrier at those who pressured me or at myself. Even though it was my own choice, it felt like such an invasion of privacy, of space, of soul. I was violated and ashamed but was afraid I wouldn't be able to pay my rent if I lost my job.

I did not feel like a dancer. I was a hungry soul trying to make ends meet and pursuing my dream with no wise counsel in sight. I fell to temptation that was urged on by the surroundings and friends I had chosen. (To this day, I always tell my kids that it takes just one friend to steer us off in the wrong direction. How I pray they learn that lesson a less painful way than I did!)

One night, the owner called on my night off and said, "Sunny, a client is requesting you." The owner never wanted to send a customer away unsatisfied and unhappy. So I grudgingly arrived at the bar. The client showed up in his red Ferrari and paid me $3,000 to hang out with him all night, sipping drinks in the back room. Sadly, he, like many other millionaires with a wife and kids at home, did this all the time. They could afford to pay beautiful women to be their companions, dates, escorts. Money meant nothing to them. Did their families mean nothing as well? It troubled my heart deeply.

As we talked backstage, I learned that the girls I worked with all had their own reasons for choosing this job. Some of them seemed like women you'd run into anywhere. Several were putting themselves through college—including a businesswoman who had gone back to college for a degree and saw this as the best way to pay her tuition. Another was putting herself through med school. There were single moms just trying to survive, career dancers who loved what they did, and druggies living from paycheck to paycheck. And there were some who, like me, really didn't want to be there but believed it was an effective way to pay their rent and pursue their dreams. It was the best money we could make in a job that allowed greater flexibility than anything else we were likely to find.

The clientele represented many segments of society. We had wild, lust-filled college boys and rheumy-eyed eighty-year-old men. Blue-collar workers and wealthy execs. Men who wanted to touch, and men who just wanted to watch. And men who threw money our way as if it were confetti. Like Mark. I had quite a painful incident with him. He and I had sometimes chatted during my breaks, and he'd seemed like a sweet guy at the time. He was tall, with chiseled good looks that could have made him Leonardo DiCaprio's brother. Mark would throw $100 bills on the stage. (Talk about a red flag I missed—why would a sweet guy hang out at a bikini bar throwing money around? What *was* I thinking?) The chats developed into after-hours meals, which led to dating off and on. Nothing serious, but I must admit we slept together one time. He dropped in and out of sight over time, sometimes for weeks, before reappearing. One morning, not long after I had slept with him, I woke up with some scary symptoms that required a trip to the doctor.

I asked him to go with me, and while we were sitting side by side in the waiting room, he simply stood up and left. He never returned. I called him and left messages, but not a word back. A little while later, I confided in a coworker at the bar.

"Sunny," she said, calling me by my stage name, "you don't want that man to call you back. You do know he's a meth dealer, don't you?" The look on my face told her the obvious answer was no. I'd been clueless. A few months later, he called and left me a message to call him—a message I never bothered to answer.

I was shaken that I'd been so naive. It was a deeply painful lesson for a young girl in her first months in Los Angeles. Little did I know that years later I would pay an even greater price for my lack of judgment.

I have many situations in my past that are left unfinished and unspoken—now simply scars on my heart that only God can heal.

It was at the bikini bar that I also first learned about sugar daddies— men who give financial and material support to younger women in exchange for sexual favors. At one level, it was practical. Sure, these girls had the cars and clothes and rent they needed. But they also had to give more of themselves than I ever wanted to give. It is here, again, that I see God's hand of protection in my life. The things in life I was desperate for—love, attention, material provision—seemed on the surface to be provided in these relationships. But I did know I wanted more. Although I wanted to be an actor as my career, I wanted my home life, my intimate life, to be real and based on actual relationship. I wanted real laughter—not forced. Real conversations that went deep. Real connection that genuinely cared about one another's needs. Clearly, a sugar daddy couldn't provide those.

For those subconscious, God-given reasons, I struggled with the job from the first day, and it never got easier. I may have lacked the moral compass that should have kept me out of there in the first place, but somewhere inside, I still had the capacity for shame—a feeling that exploded in me each time I stepped into the club. I had worked in retail selling things, and now I realized that my job wasn't acting at all—it was selling myself. My shame grew into a dark cloud and began taking a toll I would not recognize for some time to come.

So many things that God created for all of us were deeply imbedded within me, and I am so grateful that God kept those ideals clear so I could easily avoid even the sweetest sugar daddy. I admit, I had many of them cross my path those few years, but I never gave in to their manipulation. I would later find that my heavenly Daddy wouldn't love me only while I was young and beautiful, but forever. My Daddy wouldn't use money as a bribe. Instead, he would move heaven and earth—and even use the radio—to get my attention.

CHASING MY DREAM

The months I worked at the bikini bar would have been unremittingly bleak except for the acting classes I began taking the day I moved to L.A.

I loved them! Taking on a role, portraying a persona, to tell a story that somehow reflected our common human experience made me feel alive and connected like nothing else I had ever done. I lived for those classes at the Tracy Roberts Actors Studio on Ventura Boulevard in Studio City.

One class was taught by Tracy Roberts and another by acting coach Bobby Garabedian. Bobby's teaching strengthened my resolve and dream to act. I was growing more sure each day that this was the dream I was meant to pursue.

But so many other people had the same dream! It seemed everyone in the greater Los Angeles area was pursuing acting or modeling, yet there were so few good opportunities. If you wanted even a bit part, you had to get headshots photographed by professionals and submitted through an agent. Studios flipped through these black-and-white 8-by-10s like a card dealer in Vegas—quickly and without emotion. Auditions—if you were lucky enough to pass the card-dealer test—were humiliating. A hundred other people who looked just like you milled around, waiting for their turn to stand in front of the casting director, producers, and/or camera and recite lines—each person hoping they had that tiny edge that would make them stand out in this room of clones.

A grapevine of sorts delivered news of projects looking for cast members or extras. I was fortunate on rare occasions to land parts in music videos. Before I could blink, the day after I moved to L.A., Sarah got me a spot as a topless background girl in a film she did, and I jumped at it for fear of not being able to pay my first month's rent. I didn't even take the time to think twice about it—I just knew I needed to pay my share of the rent, which was something I worried about frequently. Afterward, even though I made $500, I felt horrified. I had been thrown into a sick circle that would now try to suck me in even deeper.

Another time, Olivia, my other roommate, had booked a job and offered to include me. It turned out to be a nude photo shoot with a photographer who shot in the style of *Playboy*—very Marilyn Monroe-ish and classic. But after my photo shoot, I begged them to destroy the photos. I felt sickened and disgusted with myself. It was as if I had a "good cop/ bad cop" battle in my mind over how appropriate or inappropriate nude photography was in the modeling industry. The good cop won that day. I am incredibly thankful they honored my request!

I didn't want to be a Playboy Playmate, and yet I did want it. I wanted what I saw as significance, and those in the Playboy circle definitely got it in industry respect. I didn't want to be a stripper. What I really wanted—desperately wanted—was to be an actor. I wanted to be perfect, beautiful, respected, and adored. What was wrong with me? Why wasn't I one of the young girls who seemed to effortlessly land the sought-after roles? Hello, J. J. Abrams! Is a lead in *Mission Impossible* too much to ask?

I contracted with several agents, but I discovered you get lost in the shuffle. None of my agents gave me any guidance on how to make it all work. In fact, a few male agents and managers dropped me when they realized I wouldn't sleep with them after hanging out with them on weekends.

I didn't understand then why I couldn't land a solid, rewarding acting job, but I know now. God had a plan, and he was working it out even then, when I was clueless.

Chapter 8

HUNGRY HEART

As the deer pants for streams of water,
    so my soul pants for you, my God.
My soul thirsts for God, for the living God.
    When can I go and meet with God?
PSALM 42:1–2

I had left San Diego to become an actor but so far had found myself dancing at a bikini bar and socializing at the Playboy Mansion. Was I on the road to success, or had I taken a wrong turn along the way? I honestly wasn't sure. Maybe these were avenues toward my destination, and by traveling them, I'd make the money and connections I needed for my life of acting lessons and auditions and finding my place in the Hollywood entertainment world. I hoped so. But I hadn't anticipated finding myself in such places—no more than I'd anticipated what was about to come. I might have thought I was in the driver's seat, but Someone Else was directing traffic.

How appropriate that God would use my acting coach to begin to steer me in the right direction. I had tremendous respect for Bobby Garabedian, not only because of his skills (he was an Oscar nominee and the holder of numerous industry awards), but also because he was so personable and genuine. Sarah and I began taking his class in August

1998 and often chatted with Bobby after class. I soon came to think of him as not only a coach but also a friend.

More than once, Bobby invited us to come to the church he attended, Malibu Vineyard.

"Hey, how about this Sunday?" he asked one day, looking hopefully from me to Sarah. "I'd love for you to see what Elkin (his wife) and the kids love about the place."

I agreed to think about it. Not because I had any interest in church—which represented dull, irrelevant religion in my eyes—but because when Bobby spoke about his family loving the place, I was drawn to the idea of having a wholesome place to go that I could love. The closest thing I had to that was partying at the Playboy Mansion.

At the next mansion party, Hef overheard Sarah and me talking about it and said, "How cute—so you girls want to go to a church? I'll send a limo so you can go in style." I wish I could have seen the shocked expression on my face. It was another glimpse of Hef's mysterious complexity—this time, I saw his fatherly side. His motivation seemed to be nothing other than to make us happy, and if we thought a trip to church sounded like fun, he was all for it. What a quirky adventure it would be! Riding in a Playboy limo to church—who could turn *that* down? Leave it to Hef. Every time you tried to put him in a box and define him, he'd do something outlandish to prove that no one truly knew the real Hugh Hefner.

Or maybe I should say, "Leave it to God to defy our efforts to fit him into any box." His choice to use Hugh Hefner—Mr. Playboy himself—to get me to a church service shows how creative and outside-the-box our Creator can be.

Right on schedule the next Sunday morning, a black stretch limo appeared in front of our house. We were giggling as the well-tailored chauffer opened the door for us, and then off we went, chilling in luxury while chatting about hair extensions, the latest workout, what to pick up from Starbucks on the way, and what the "church people" would think when we drove up. To us, this was a fun little outing—an adventure born out of curiosity. We didn't expect anything profound out of it.

Malibu Vineyard was about an hour from our house, in a little area of Malibu near Cross Creek—one of those quaint shopping areas with a mix of retail, office buildings, and cozy places to eat. Our limo rolled down Cross Creek, turned onto a modest side street that likely had never had a limo on it before, and parked in front of a brown, single-story school building. "This is it?" Sarah asked, peering out the window. "It doesn't look like any church I've ever seen. There's not even a cross on it."

"Bobby said they meet in a school." I checked the address on the lined yellow paper Bobby had given me. "Yeah, this is it. Webster Elementary."

We shouldn't have had any doubts we were in the right place, judging from the number of cars pulling into the parking lot and all the people gathering in groups outside the entrance doors and chatting enthusiastically. Who else would be at a school on a Sunday morning? Especially people of all ages and entire families, some carrying Bibles. As it turned out, I don't recall any heads turning when we climbed out of the limo and headed inside. Go figure. I guess nothing's a surprise when you live in Southern California.

The interior was no more remarkable than the exterior. We stepped into a bland all-purpose room with rows of gray metal folding chairs facing a small stage where a band was tuning up their instruments. A drummer tapped a rapid sequence on his drums as though testing the sound in the big room. Drums rather than an organ? Clearly this wasn't going to be the same kind of church music I heard as a child at either of my grandparents' churches.

Sarah and I found Bobby, and he introduced us to Elkin and their two kids. What a perfect fit they seemed to be—their bond of love seemed palpable. The chairs filled up quickly, and I was a little surprised at how casually everyone was dressed—jeans, shorts, and flip-flops—just like the people milling around at a mall.

I was impressed with the quality of the musicians, but didn't sing along, even though the words were printed on a screen over the stage. Sarah stood looking around—her beautiful wavy blonde hair swishing as she craned her neck to see everyone around us—as though she were searching for someone. I knew that look. I saw it anytime we were in public. She was assessing the people around us. Who might be famous? She was adept at scoping out a crowd while at the same time making the people she was with feel they were special and had her attention—a skill honed by years of working the crowd at the mansion.

As the band played, people raised their hands or clapped or swayed like their bodies and souls were caught up in the meaning of the words—acting like you would at a concert of a favorite musician singing her huge hit song. This was definitely not my grandparents' church! These people weren't simply going through the motions of religion; they were immersed in the experience. Some even shouted out, "Hallelujah!" or "Thank you, Jesus!" I thought, *How dear. These people are really into this.*

I didn't look down on them for it. In fact, I would have loved to feel what they felt, but I didn't feel anything at all. I was simply observing a group of people who seemed to be on the same page—a God page—a page I'd never really had in my book. God had just never been part of my story. I don't remember a thing about the sermon, except that a likable guy got up to the podium and spoke. My mind wandered, and I mostly watched interactions between families. They all seemed so *connected.* Then more music, and it was over. At Bobby's invitation, we joined him, Elkin, and their children family as they grabbed a bite to eat. After a round of good-bye hugs, Sarah and I chatted a bit.

"Did you like it?" I asked Sarah.

"It was okay. I don't know if I'll go back, though. How about you?"

"I don't think so. But it was sweet," I said. I felt that I was living out my dream and was convinced that life was good just as it was. I didn't "need" church in my life.

The driver picked us up at the school at precisely the time we had asked him to. And it was on to whatever came next.

A HOLLYWOOD INSIDER

The Playboy Mansion parties had become a regular part of my life. I was fascinated with the guests—some were so intriguing. Lots of them were famous—some were nice, and some aloof. I'd gotten used to kicking back with a drink near the pool on the soft, lovely evenings that seem to happen only in Southern California. One Saturday, a guy sipping a glass of vodka came over and took the seat Sarah had just vacated. He had shaggy blond hair that kept falling in his face. He looked vaguely familiar. It took me a moment before I recognized him. "Hey," he said with self-confidence, "I'm David."

"Hi, David. I'm Andrea."

We flirted for a few minutes. I remember he made me laugh. Truly he was a charming man in a quirky, funny way. He seemed to assume I knew who he was, so I kept him guessing whether I did or didn't. But I *did*—David Spade, a regular on *Saturday Night Live* with a number of movies on his résumé, and the star of a top-rated TV show called *Just Shoot Me!* He asked for my phone number, but I wouldn't give it to him, and after chatting for a while, he drifted on. I didn't think much about it afterward. Evenings at the mansion were like that. You'd have a great conversation with someone you'd never see again. Or you'd have an odd conversation with someone who, five minutes later, wouldn't remember they had ever met you, because they were too strung out on something.

As it turned out, I did see him again. At party after party he kept coming over to chat with me, and we would hang out—walking through the gardens, laughing at the spider monkeys, checking out the movie that was showing in the mansion's theatre.

He pursued me until I finally gave in and we started dating. Sometimes I'd visit the set of his TV show, enjoying the flurry of activity of the cast and crew behind the scenes. It was fun becoming a Hollywood insider. This was the world I hoped to find a place in for myself.

David lived part-time in Arizona, where he had family, and once he flew me there to hang out with him for a weekend. He was the first guy who took me on dates by plane. Exciting, to say the least! He wouldn't be the last.

ON MY OWN AGAIN

After ten long months (it felt like so much longer), my work at the bar hadn't become any less objectionable. In fact, my feelings of disgust had grown. On the drive to work, the familiar sick feeling inside me would grow steadily worse, so that just the mere act of pushing the door open to enter was becoming intolerable. I hated the feeling that I was selling myself, and finally, I reached a point where I knew I just couldn't act the part anymore. It had been nice not to have to worry about having what I needed to pay my bills, and the money I'd been saving in my dresser drawer was adding up. But I *had* to escape the seediness. I was yearning for something, but I was no longer willing to do this job to find it.

How had I even fallen for this in the first place? I was angry with myself for being so gullible that I would stoop to such a low way of earning money to pay my rent and make ends meet as I waited to make it in Hollywood. Ugh! It wasn't worth this. What was I really chasing, anyway? A successful acting career? Stardom? Wealth? Or maybe just work I could enjoy while honing my acting skills. I wasn't as sure as I had once been. Whatever it was, it surely was *not* this. So I simply quit. On to the next thing, whatever that would be, to bring me closer to my dream.

Two months after I quit the bikini bar, the owners of the North Hollywood house where Sarah, Olivia, and I lived put it up for sale, and we had to move. I had enjoyed living with them, but I was feeling a drive to push myself to live on my own. Not only did I want the satisfaction of feeling independent; as I look back now, I suspect I was also trying to guard against being persuaded to turn back to ways of making a living that I found uncomfortable. I was afraid that if they tried to persuade me to take that kind of work, I would be unable to hold my ground and would give in. The pleaser in me that wanted to avoid conflict and just feel accepted might prove to be more powerful than my desire to stand my already shaky ground.

In July 1999, I chose a one-bedroom apartment in Hollywood on Sunset and Cherokee. Transvestites and drag queens hung out right around the corner. My rent went up to $675, but I figured that for the next year, I could live off the $14,000 cash I had stashed in my dresser drawer—hoping then to supplement that with what I might be able to earn doing a small acting or modeling job here or there. I wanted to focus more on acting, and I knew it would mean I'd have to make time for more auditions and keep taking my acting classes.

Occasionally my dad and brother Josh would drive up from San Diego, where Josh was still living with Dad. My brother Jason by this time was living in Arizona, so we talked on the phone fairly regularly. It felt good to connect with the three of them, especially now that I was living alone. Mom and I spoke by phone as well. We weren't as close as I was to Dad and my brothers, but the contact was important to me.

David Spade and I continued to date off and on. Over time, I noticed that he often seemed drawn to young blonde Playmates. Did he really enjoy *me*, or was I simply the charm on his arm? I enjoyed him and his ability to make me laugh, but I just didn't see us going anywhere long term. So when I moved to my Hollywood apartment, I didn't tell him where I was going, intentionally losing touch with him. Yes, it was the conflict-avoiding people pleaser at work.

I heard through the grapevine that David had been calling around and asking about me, even calling my brother and saying, "Hey, Jason, can you give me Andrea's new number?"

My brother never told him where I was living, knowing that if I chose to disappear from a man's life, I had my reasons. It was flattering to know that David was trying to find me, but I just didn't see a relationship with him as part of the picture. I do see the irony here, as I had no clear "picture" of whatever it was I was looking for.

CONSTANT CRAVING

I'd thought having my own apartment would be a welcome achievement. I hadn't thought about the fact that I wasn't used to having a house to myself. Even as a kid, though I often felt alone, parents or siblings were in and out all around me. And when I had roommates, I'd enjoyed the casual comfort of having friends around. Also, they and their friends were in and out at random times, so I had grown accustomed to returning from work and hanging out, talking and laughing as we all tried to figure out life together. What they didn't know, however, was that I never felt the freedom just to be myself with them. I was always at work presenting myself in the way I thought they would most approve of, trying to seem more sophisticated than I really felt. To me they seemed so experienced and hip. By comparison, I felt inadequate, and because I was trying to be what I assumed they wanted me to be, I felt like the fake I was.

But in my own place, there was no one to walk through the house, dropping keys, a purse, and shoes along the way. No one who might pop her head into my bedroom to see if I wanted to share a meal, watch TV or a movie, or go out somewhere. No one using the bathroom when I wanted to use it. (Well, okay, that part was nice!) This place was quiet. Just quiet. It was a whole new world. And to my surprise, a lonely one.

Fortunately, there was a place where I could escape the loneliness. The mansion. On my way to the parties, I soothed myself that I was "living the dream" and actually had a shot at this Hollywood life. I was still taking acting lessons and making lots of connections. Slim though the chances might be, I was determined not to give up on making my aspirations a reality.

But gradually, I couldn't deny that I was also beginning to consider the parties at the mansion in a new light. I'd been noticing how empty and unsatisfying the lives of those who had already attained those things I sought seemed to be. What if they were showing up at the mansion just to look for ever more extreme diversions from their own emptiness? One of the rooms, the game room I believe, had a mirrored ceiling. What a telling sign that many of us hanging out there were seeking to see ourselves look happy and successful with the rich and the famous. But mirrors can't reflect the emptiness of the heart.

I'd spent a year trying to live like all the cool people I knew. Like the people who hung out with Hef—pursuing extravagance, sexual pleasures, drugs, and partying. But ultimately it now seemed that so many seemed driven by a desire to escape. And I'd been trying to be like the friends of Sarah and Olivia, who were pursuing acting, incessantly running to acting classes and auditions, hoping for the big break that might catapult them to success—working other jobs in their spare time to try to make ends meet. None of them seemed to be living in satisfaction, completeness, or contentment. And I certainly wasn't.

What I had expected to be the time of my life was turning out to be just dark, empty, and confusing. I had so much of what others on the "outside" wanted. After all, to someone new to "the system," it can be a dream come true to have a standing invitation to the mansion. But even if that was impressive, it wasn't remotely enough to bring the satisfaction in life I was looking for. There was something more to experience in life—something better. I knew it. I longed for it. I craved it.

I had to fill up all those empty, lonely hours in my apartment with something, so I went back to the thing that gave me comfort—emotional eating. Just like the little girl I'd been when I hit the pantry after school and delighted in the food at the Moores' house and at my grandparents' houses, I still interpreted food as the comforting evidence of love and belonging. In the absence of the camaraderie of meaningful relationships, I craved food as my substitute.

The longer I lived alone, the lonelier and more stressed I got, and my long-term obsessions with food, athleticism, and health quickly resurfaced. After all, those issues had never been resolved; they had just been pushed into the background during all the change and activity of the past year or so since I'd moved to L.A. I'd sit at home alone on Friday nights and watch TV and eat whatever brought comfort, just as I had comforted myself as a little girl after school when my mom wasn't around. When I first moved into my apartment, I weighed about ninety pounds—my bikini bar weight. Now I started gradually putting on weight, eventually about fifteen pounds over the year.

In contrast, I also dove into research, reading hundreds of self-help books on health and wholeness, motivation and well-being, foods, fad diets, and alternative medicine. This quest simply fed into my ongoing obsessive food control—something that had continued to be a part of my everyday life. It had lingered from the days of living with my dad, ebbed and flowed in my time at Sarah's, and now moved more to the forefront of my thinking as I lived alone. Looking back, I clearly see that my inner hunger, my heart hunger for something real, was driving me to find ways to fill myself, but none of them were working. Certainly not the indulging in comfort foods or the latest food fad.

What else could work? Becoming famous? Not yet! Rich? Far from reality. A steady career immersed in the craft of acting? That was costing me more money than I was making. So I just kept reading self-help books voraciously, latching on to and trying one idea after the next, but finding none of them satisfying.

When I wasn't obsessing over what I was or wasn't eating, depression would surface, warning me that it had been lurking in the shadows all along. I wanted desperately to prevent that ominous darkness. Constant preoccupation with food and self-improvement was the distraction I used to escape the darkness. It was the only way I knew to prevent the shadows from moving in and taking over.

Meanwhile I was realizing my dwindling $14,000 wouldn't last forever. I needed to find steady, dependable work. Besides, work would help stave off depression, I reasoned. I booked jobs here and there—modeling for a jeans designer, guest starring on some TV shows. But no matter how hard I tried, I couldn't land consistent acting work or free myself from the stress of always looking for and chasing the next best job.

By this time, I'd become aware that most young actors trying to break into the movies face these same challenges, and if they don't go the route of such things as stripping, doing nude photo shoots, or working for escort services (something I never did), they have to get extra creative for their income sources: walking dogs, party planning, house cleaning, nannying, gardening, tending bar, and more. Like so many before me, I couldn't figure out how to get to the top of the Hollywood "It List," and I certainly wasn't willing to sleep my way to the top. Since I was a people pleaser and a bad liar, that combination would have made it nearly impossible for me to use and manipulate people to get what I wanted. I was a conflict avoider who wasn't adept at the art of selling myself, and I was too relationally transparent to hustle people to get ahead.

As excited as I had been when I'd first gained entrance to that stratosphere of Hollywood society, I eventually knew beyond a doubt that the Playboy Mansion had nothing to offer that could touch the soul hunger that marked every moment of my life. Even so, I kept going to the mansion parties.

I didn't feel ready to let go of that one constant in my life before I had something else to replace it with. I was craving something more than mere fun and diversion, something more than food and health, something more than celebrity. But what?

WHISPERS FROM GOD

Soul hunger or not, a girl—especially a wannabe actor—can't live in Los Angeles without getting her nails done. So I religiously took my place in a chair at the nail salon. Since I was earning nothing and trying to live on a shoestring, that tells you where my priorities were for how I spent my money.

One day as I sat in the black faux leather chair letting my nails dry, I picked up a well-read *Ladies' Home Journal*. (I would have rather read *People*, but couldn't find one on the rack.) There was a teaser on the cover, something about a diet that really works. Always conscious of every pound and inch, I was curious and flipped directly to the article and read it.

Then I read it again. Carefully.

It spoke about a diet that used prayer to tap into weight control. "God made your body, and God can help you win the battle against overeating." I read on to see how the diet combined healthy eating with a spiritual understanding of our bodies and our innermost person. The program incorporated daily prayer, confession, and, of all things, Bible reading. Something stirred in me. It was almost as if the article had pulled back the curtain to peer into that deep place in my soul, the place from which my hunger was coming. I knew I was reading truth. There *was* a link between my soul and food.

The article contained a reference to a website, so I left the salon, went back to my lonely apartment, and ordered the CDs and daily devotions so I could start the daily practices the article had recommended. I began to keep a journal and read the prayers and Bible verses daily—a practice that was new to me. As I did, I felt a stirring of excitement deep inside. The more I prayed and the more Bible verses I read, the more I sensed that not only was my own heart awakened, but somehow, a power from outside me—something I did not understand—was beginning to flow *into* me. I didn't know how to describe it: mystical, supernatural, spiritual? I wasn't sure. My obsession with controlling food began to ease as I replaced my recurring thoughts of food with Bible verses and prayers. I actually began to see progress.

One day I was sitting in my apartment paying bills, and I started to panic about my upcoming car payment. My first instinct kicked in: I bolted for the kitchen to grab something sweet. Suddenly, I stopped and said, "God, if this prayer stuff really works, I'm coming to you first." The urge to eat passed, and I went back to my task. Within a day, a check arrived for a small job I'd recently done. Car payment covered!

Whoa, this was so awesome! Maybe this was what religious people meant when they talked about "getting in touch with God." I thought of the many musicians and actors over the years known for their experimentation with Eastern mysticism, meditation, Scientology, and being born again. Like Bobby, my acting coach, whose faith was a huge part of his family's life. There really was something to this spiritual stuff. I went to a local bookstore and bought my very first Bible. A pink one!

Through prayer and Bible reading, for the first time in my life I began to understand how empty my heart felt. Hollow. And I was beginning to grasp that I wasn't hungry for food; I was hungry for this emptiness to be filled. I longed for freedom from my food issues and my own dark emotions, and it seemed that spiritual truth just might be the pathway toward healing I was looking for.

On the website for the weight program, I noticed that a church in Burbank hosted a study group. I got up the nerve and just showed up one evening. I liked it. Most of the women in the group were older than me, and some certainly knew a lot more about God and the Bible than I did, but to my amazement, they welcomed me like a new friend. I knew then and there I'd be back the following week.

The women were kind to me. I'd never sat in a circle and had people pray to God *for me*. As they prayed, tears ran down my cheeks, though I wasn't sure exactly why. Their prayers made me feel cared for and encouraged as if I, Andrea Logan, mattered personally to them and to God. While they all enjoyed discussing passages of the Bible, I usually had no understanding of what they were discussing. And because I wanted to belong and contribute, I started to read my Bible more.

It's fascinating now to look back and see so clearly what I totally missed at the time.

Without even realizing it, I had taken several significant steps to remove a multitude of distracting, confusing, and unhealthy voices in my life. By quitting the bikini bar, I'd removed the disgusting, often vile messages (spoken and unspoken) from the men eyeing my dancing body on the stage. By moving into my own apartment, I'd removed the values of my roommates that seemed to conflict with mine. Now in the silence inhabiting the space those voices had occupied, I was hearing the whispers of God.

Even so, at this point my spiritual exploration was a means to an end. I saw it as self-help to make my life happier, healthier, and more satisfying. Fortunately, God isn't limited by our naïveté, nor is he thwarted by our self-centered purposes. He was accomplishing his purposes though the power of his Word, no matter what my purposes were.

ENEMY ON THE PROWL

The weight-loss program and the Bible study meetings at the church were new and exciting developments in my life, but I was still dragging a lot of baggage with me—especially my three biggest issues.

I was still wearing my scars of abandonment and aching to belong.

I was still hearing the voices of never being enough.

I was still carrying my anger that demanded I alone must have complete control over my life.

My battle with food issues, I was discovering through the weight-loss program, was tied in with all three. God was using my free time to break through my defenses so that I would hear his voice. I was beginning to tune in to his voice, though in all honesty, I had no comprehension of just whose voice this was.

I had no clear understanding of God—I thought of him as God up in the sky somewhere, but he seemed unreachable. In L.A., God is "everywhere," with a lot of self-idolatry and New Age thinking in the mix. I had no connection to our Creator. And though the weight-loss program used prayer and Bible reading, it had not clearly made a case for surrendering my life to Jesus Christ—a concept I didn't know or understand. As far as I was concerned, I was trying out these spiritual tactics to see if they would give me control over my food issues.

To give *me* control!

Unbeknownst to me, not only did I have God, the creator of the universe who knew me by name and loved me unconditionally, but I also had an enemy who had been getting quite a free ride in my life. First Peter 5:8 reads, "Be alert and of sober mind. Your enemy the devil prowls around like a roaring lion looking for someone to devour." In the choices I'd been making, I had been setting myself up as an easy target.

If I had understood that there were spiritual forces at war over my soul, I might have anticipated that my enemy was about to try out some tactics of his own that would ultimately give him control over me. He was about to send a parade of distractions marching through my life—distractions that would keep my attention anywhere else but on God's voice.

He would tap into my feelings of abandonment, luring me into a false sense of belonging where I did not really belong.

He would quiet my voices of never being enough with empty words of flattery and promises of affection.

He would tap into my anger and my need for control, luring me to leap blindly headlong into self-destructive directions with no regard for or awareness of any moral authority above me.

Wrap those all up and follow them to their natural conclusions, and they will lead me to only one place: LOST.

But I didn't know that yet. I was still certain I could find a place to belong. I was still trying to silence the self-defeating voices by proving my value and worth though my performance. And I was still fighting the only way I knew how—through self-sufficiency and a drive to control my circumstances.

Even if it meant driving headlong into a collision with disaster.

Chapter 9

ALLURING DISTRACTIONS

> When tempted, no one should say, "God is tempting me."
> For God cannot be tempted by evil, nor does he tempt any-
> one; but each person is tempted when they are dragged
> away by their own evil desire and enticed. Then, after
> desire has conceived, it gives birth to sin; and sin, when
> it is full-grown, gives birth to death.
>
> JAMES 1:13–15

A parade of alluring distractions was about to begin. How appropriate, given my driven need to belong and have my value affirmed, that my enemy chose to lead that parade with men. I'll say it now—these next few chapters are painful to write. But unless I'm open and transparent here, the transformation—and struggle—that lies ahead will not be understood fully.

Men, it seemed to me, began coming from all directions. One day when I was doing laundry at the machines in the apartment complex, a rather goofy guy introduced himself—I'll call him Cat Guy. He loved cats—and lots of them. Cat Guy took up the habit of knocking on my door at all times of the night. He must have been nocturnal, like all his four-legged roommates in his somewhat smelly apartment. Then there was Cute Guy—a friend of Cat Guy—who wanted to be oh-so-friendly with me. I did my best to be neighborly, but made it clear I wasn't interested. In a nearby apartment lived Jeans Designer Guy, who, though married, wasn't shy about hitting on me. It must have been my awesome teal Isuzu that drew these guys to me, you think? Or maybe a secret underground apartment newsletter that announced the moving in of every new single woman!

Enter Blake, a guy in his mid-twenties, born and raised in Beverly Hills. The son of a successful businessman, he planned to follow in his father's footsteps and was attending an elite school when we met. But that's not what attracted me. Blake was so much fun. A great conversationalist who was intelligent and witty, just being with him kept me smiling and laughing—something I desperately needed during this lonely time. He pursued me—a wonderful feeling to a girl who longs to belong. I was flattered.

Blake lived in an expensive apartment in the Wilshire Corridor, an exclusive area near Century City and the Fox and MGM studios. Farrah Fawcett lived nearby, and Charlie Sheen lived in the same building as Blake. Occasionally I would run into Charlie at the building with Blake—and I was impressed by what a nice guy he was. Soon a portion of my free time became Blake time—delightful dates that left me feeling special and important. There was a problem, however. He enjoyed recreational drugs and tended to drink too much. I chose not to make an issue out of it and behaved as if it didn't bother me, even though it did. Once again, my desire to matter, to feel a sense of belonging, overcame my self-respect, values, and comfort zone.

Around this time, I met Jenni, a vivacious brunette who was one year older than me and had a huge social circle. She seemed to be going places in the pursuit of her acting career. Jenni and I met on a music video shoot and hit it off. Before long, we both landed enviable spots in a music video by Kid Rock. We were the main girls among many on the shoot and got to stand next to him for several shots. How many times had I hoped for that during this season? Too many to count! With each job, I had the hope of connecting with someone bigger who would in turn help connect me to the next level of my career. This is how the industry works. (Oh, how I don't miss those times of dealing with high hopes of the next job catapulting me to be the "it girl" in Hollywood!)

In the end, when watching the video, I realized with a thud in my heart how hard it was to even pick me out among all the other skinny blondes parading around the star. It did lead to a few other video spots—including one for the band Creed—but nothing that catapulted me into any substantial acting jobs.

Minor modeling and acting jobs came and went as quickly as the men. I was drifting from one relationship and job to another, hoping for something solid to take me to the next level. Instead, I was going in circles. Blake, whose use of drugs and alcohol were intensifying, had been moving in and out of my life. For a few months, he even disappeared without a word.

A DOSE OF HARSH REALITY

Then Blake oozed back into my life, and by this time, I could see he was enjoying cocaine and alcohol more than he was enjoying me. He'd been in and out of Alcoholics Anonymous before and during our relationship, and clearly he was out at this time.

One night Blake came to my apartment with cocaine. I had tried it before (and other drugs too), but I didn't want cocaine that night. It scared me.

"Andrea, you've got to try this. Come on. It's amazing."

Looking for an easy way to avoid conflict, I waved him off and tried to change the subject, but he was relentless. Over and over, like a squeaky wheel, he cajoled, begged, pouted, and pleaded until finally I caved. There may be no more telling picture of my desperation for acceptance than the image I carry of me, heart hammering with fear, despising the act I was doing, snorting cocaine.

I still weighed less than a hundred pounds at the time, my metabolism no doubt weakened by the eating disorder over the years. Yet, as is true for most people who do drugs, neither of us gave any thought to how the drug's potency would affect me at that weight.

Soon after snorting the cocaine, my chest grew tighter and tighter, and I began to panic. Within minutes, I could barely breathe.

"Call 9-1-1!" I said, gasping.

"We can't!" Blake shouted, running his fingers through his hair and beginning to pace. "We can't." He started to freak out, wringing his hands, walking in circles in my apartment, watching me. "We'll get arrested."

Talk about a moment of instant clarity! I couldn't breathe, and he cared more about his legal risk? I don't know which hurt more—being unable to breathe, the fear of dying, or the lightning bolt of realization that this man didn't care about me at all.

"I don't care." My voice was scared and angry. "I can't breathe. I'm dying. Call 9-1-1. I'm having a heart attack!" I looked at him, pleading, weeping now in desperation and terror. "I don't want to die!" He grabbed the unused coke, ran to the bathroom, and flushed it down the toilet— and *then* he made the call.

Within moments, a couple cops and a couple EMTs showed up. Blake let them in, and as so many addicts do, he pretended to be sober and came up with a clever story.

"Someone, I don't know who, gave her this cocaine," he whined.

I said nothing—I was just lying on the floor trying to breathe.

The bigger EMT was angry. "What did you think you were doing?" he spat out as he squatted down beside me. He slammed the blood pressure cuff around my arm and yanked it closed. "Stop breathing so hard if you're dying," he said sarcastically as he pumped up the cuff, held a stethoscope to my arm, and listened, continuing to mutter angrily. He glanced at the two cops, who had been sitting beside me asking occasional questions. Something unspoken passed between them.

"Look," one of the cops said gently, "just lie still and try to relax. Take slow, deep breaths." He demonstrated, helping me pace my breathing. By this time, Blake was pacing a greater and greater distance away from us.

"It's like you just had way, way, *way* too much caffeine," the other one said, calmly and gently. "Your heart is just accelerated, and that's why it's harder to breathe."

The first cop, who reminded me of my cop father, said, "We can take you to the hospital if you want, but then you'll have an overdose on your record." He put a kind hand on my trembling arm. "Or we can just sit here with you until you come down from this."

"Unless you get worse," the second cop said, "and then we'll have to take you to the hospital."

I nodded, overwhelmed by their kindness. The two EMTs packed up their equipment and left, the angry one grumbling all the way out the door. Blake, eager not to spend any more time with two cops, waved good-bye from across the room and used the opportunity to make his less-than-gallant escape.

But I was not left alone. Those two kind policemen sat by my side and kept me calm for more than an hour until my heart rate and breathing finally returned to normal.

Angels unaware? Most certainly a divine appointment—a foretaste of what was to come. To this day, my heart still fills at the thought of those two uniformed policemen staying by my side, and I am grateful beyond words for their calm, protective presence that helped me genuinely sense that God was watching over me.

You would have thought that this experience would have stirred my interest in returning to the spiritual exploration I had begun, but by now, the faith-based diet had completely faded from my life. It wasn't that

I didn't still think it was a good program and a positive force in my life; I'd just become too distracted, too drained, too confused, too busy trying to make a living and find people who made me feel like I mattered. How could I stay with it when there was so much else going on?

You'd also think I would have dumped Blake immediately, and the fact that I didn't glaringly illustrates how muddled my judgment had become. Even though I knew our relationship was toxic, I just couldn't face the conflict of a breakup. It would be a few more months before I found the strength to end it.

Meanwhile, the odd jobs took my mind off my loneliness, and they often dangled the potential of connections with Hollywood insiders that might lead to my big break. But I was in a growing funk that was growing deeper in a hurry. My hunger wasn't being satisfied. The hole inside was gnawing at me, and I couldn't find the way to fill it.

By July 2000, right around my birthday, I decided that eleven months of living alone was more than enough. My friendship with Jenni had grown, so we found an apartment in West Hollywood behind the Beverly Center and moved in together. My portion of the rent was $800 a month—a hefty increase over what I had been paying. Plus, I still had car payments and insurance payments to make. I tried not to think about how I was going to pay my bills, because it felt so good to be living with a person again.

The income from my odd jobs wasn't going to cover my share of the rent, so I found two steady restaurant jobs. I was a hostess at the Mondrian Restaurant, a fine, ritzy establishment with moneyed clientele, and at the other end of the spectrum, I waited tables at Doughboys on Third Street in West Hollywood, a casual neighborhood eatery known for its incredible desserts and breads. I didn't make much by Hollywood standards—$150 a day at best.

The apartment had another drawback in addition to the increase in rent, though it took me a while to figure it out. Shortly after moving in, I began to have asthma attacks. At first they were fairly mild, but I checked with a doctor, who suspected I was having an allergic reaction to something new in my environment. The only thing new was my apartment—and its brand-new carpeting that still had a fairly strong chemical smell. Soon I was sure it was true—I was allergic to my apartment. Affordable apartments, however, were hard to come by, and I wasn't about to give it up yet. I began using allergy medications and inhalers for the first time in my life, hoping they would protect me until the newness of the carpet wore off. Still, the longer I hung around my place, the less healthy I felt. I was beginning to feel I couldn't catch a break.

Meanwhile, my food control and self-help craze were intensifying, leaving me feeling that the spiritual stuff I had tried for a while hadn't worked after all. My health, rather than improving, was deteriorating. I was growing weaker again as my anorexia intensified. Pound by pound, I was losing weight, but when I looked in the mirror, I still saw a fat girl. I knew from experience that this was a symptom of the illness, but knowing it didn't change what I saw, which left me feeling even more defeated.

Between the allergic reaction, long hours at hard work, eating issues, and scrambling for money, I felt depleted and very weak. I struggled just to be able to do the jobs I was being paid for, but before long, I couldn't. I left both jobs and didn't go back. I also finally broke up with Blake.

After our breakup, my health issues flared. Stress? My unhealthy life-style catching up with me? Who knows. And to heap more pain into the mix, my asthma attacks had now become terrifying. They debilitated and weakened me in one way, and my continuing eating disorders debilitated and weakened me in another. Physically, I was a mess.

AN L.A. CLICHÉ

Some months later, feeling a bit stronger, I took a job at a small Asian sushi restaurant in Westwood. Given its small, intimate size, it was popular with the in-crowd, including celebrity regulars. It was definitely a far more tolerable crowd than the one at the bikini bar. One night, a buff guy with dark hair sat at one of my tables with a few friends. I didn't recognize him, but clearly others there did. He and his friends had a great time laughing, drinking, and gesturing wildly. I gave them sushi suggestions when asked and flirted as I usually did with everyone—just to be friendly.

The buff guy in the button-down blue shirt left me a $100 tip.

He came in a week later and introduced himself—Joe Francis. The name didn't connect with me, but my coworkers were eager to fill me in. He was the mega-rich creator of the Girls Gone Wild franchise. A lot of wealth for a guy only in his late twenties. He had started by going to college frat parties to get drunk girls to bare their breasts for the camera in exchange for a trinket, hat, or T-shirt. He moved from there to spring break venues to do the same and then launched a lucrative career making and selling videos of those "girls gone wild." (This was, of course, before his legal quagmire.)

Joe worked on me. He left me $100 tips every time he came in. So, naturally, each time I saw him come in, I thought, *Another bill paid!* But it was more than just that; it was the way he gently clasped my small hand in his giant one. "Are you sure you won't go out with me?" His voice was like velvet. His eyes danced over my face and locked on my eyes. "I'd love to spend time with you."

Eventually, as had happened so many times before, I caved.

Joe wined and dined me and treated me like a queen. We went out to eat at five-star restaurants. We never got serious, but I enjoyed the lavish dates he offered. I could laugh and let loose my goofy sense of fun and playfulness with him without feeling at all self-conscious. I was free game to do anything. Gone was the pretense of trying to act sophisticated or trendy. With him I could lightheartedly quip put-downs, dance like a goofball, and let my belly laughs come spilling out. He was simply fun, and he released that fun-loving girl who'd been getting lost in so much pain for quite a while.

On one dramatic date, Joe picked me up in his gray Lamborghini and drove me to the airport, flew me to Las Vegas, and took me to a boxing match where boxer Evander Holyfield was fighting. I even held Holyfield's robe ringside and felt so honored. Such a crazy time!

But despite that excitement, acting was still my passion—though my rare, minor roles still weren't paying the bills, and I wanted to be done with waitressing and dead-end modeling jobs. In fact, my income from waitressing was falling so far short of meeting my needs that, when another of the waitresses at the sushi restaurant taught me how to cheat the computer system and siphon off some money, thereby stealing from the restaurant, I gave in to the temptation and did it a few times.

How easily I followed the lead of my many friends. I had surrounded myself with people who were leading me in all the wrong directions, and I—who had willingly placed myself in their company—was blindly following wherever they led. It's unfathomable to me now, and, by God's grace, it is a gift to see how far I've come. How easy to forget the years I lived without the conviction of the Holy Spirit and with the lack of awareness of sin.

Maybe, I thought, *when friends warned me mockingly that I'd never make it as an actor, they were right. Am I just another failed actor wannabe, an L.A. cliché?*

But the fighter in me awakened. *I've always taken care of myself financially,* I thought, *and I always will, no matter how much of a struggle it is.* So I began to look for a skill that might lift me out of my defeat and finance my dream of becoming an actor.

I asked myself, *What in my life, other than acting, is offering me the greatest sense of satisfaction?* The answer was surprisingly easy. My fitness workouts. They provided the same stimulus that sports had provided during my high school years. Pushing my body, seeing improvement, increasing my strength.

I had been working out at a gym called LA Fitness and had become casual friends with Mike, a trainer who was also trying to be an actor. We chatted often about acting and fitness. At one point, I sensed he was interested in dating, but I made it clear to him how great it was to enjoy a friendship that wasn't a romance. He honored that and never made any advances. He did smoke pot off and on, but apart from that, he didn't party or do drugs, making him quite a contrast to the parade of friends—male and female—through my life that year.

One day at the club, I saw a flyer about a program to get certified as a personal trainer. There the fighter in me could flourish. I could have a skill instead of ceaselessly waiting tables. It sounded perfect. It appealed to my passion for fitness, my desire for lots of physical exercise to keep my weight down, and my need to earn more money than I made waiting tables.

While taking the certification, I met Scott, the owner of the fitness certification company. He was almost twenty years older than me, and I found that comforting. He became a steadying figure in my life. Not surprisingly, given my desire to be loved, it wasn't long before he and I were also dating. After earning my certification, I took a job at another gym, Crunch Fitness. I also started working for Scott in his home office, doing administrative work for his certification program.

Was I still seeing Joe? Of course.

Not to mention that Blake had begun showing up at the sushi restaurant where I was still waitressing, since I wasn't making enough money in the fitness industry yet to quit that job. Unbelievably, he was trying to rekindle the flame that had been forever snuffed out by his addictions. I made it clear I wasn't interested.

My hope of supporting myself solely as a fitness trainer led to yet another disappointment. I loved the work of training clients, but soon came to see that how much pay I received depended on how many clients I could cultivate and keep over the long haul. In essence, it was a commission job, not one that provided a steady paycheck.

I was proud of how hard I had worked without ever giving up my dream, yet I had to conclude that all I had accomplished was to add part-time trainer and part-time administrator for Scott into my already exhausting mix of bit modeling and acting jobs, all while still waiting tables. Like the great majority of women and men trying to be actors in L.A., staying afloat while chasing auditions was *not* earning me my big break.

I now faced the challenge of how to make it to auditions, given my schedule. And did I really want to go to an audition, hoping for the casting call that never seemed to come? There were so many other people with the same dream! On top of it all, I was so sick and tired of struggling with my health issues, my eating challenges, and my ever-present bone-weary fatigue. Now, more than ever before, that gnawing hunger in my soul, for reasons I did not understand, was screaming to be filled.

I had to face up to it. My determined fight to take control of my life, to find a place in this world where I could truly belong, and to silence that pervasive, self-defeating voice in my head left me with only two things: a starving body and a starving soul.

Two and a half years of living in the city of dreams, of making many choices I would not make again, of heartache and rejection. Toss in my painful years as a troubled adolescent and my year in San Diego, and in truth, for more than a decade I'd been a champion of self-destruction while striving for more on every level—more success, more happiness, more significance. They were all just as elusive as that sense of belonging I had yearned for since childhood. Despite all my efforts, my wrestling match with food issues and health saw no reprieve, and my three-year daily grind had become a deep grinding on my very soul. I was starving to be a champion at something other than bringing on more pain, but no matter what I did or how hard I tried, I could not make my life work.

I had come to a crossroads.

Chapter 10

THE STOPLIGHT

For we know, brothers and sisters loved by God, that he has chosen you, because our gospel came to you not simply with words but also with power, with the Holy Spirit and deep conviction.

1 THESSALONIANS 1:4–5

After being on my feet all day and smelling like restaurant food, I was used to coming home, peeling out of my work clothes, and hurrying off to acting class or an audition or a date with the wrong man.

It was a Monday night in late fall of 2000, when, after swapping the uniform of a waitress for the stylish look of an actor, I hurriedly locked up the apartment I shared with Jenni, slid back into my Isuzu Amigo, and headed to my private session with acting coach Christina Hart. I was using money I couldn't afford to pay for the coaching, but I told myself it was worth it if it prepared me for those hard-to-get auditions. It was my first session with her, and the location struck me as odd—a church, Hollywood Presbyterian, on the corner of Highland and Hollywood Boulevard.

My feet and back ached. I'd put in an extra-long shift at Doughboys and only had time for a quick shower and a protein bar to tide me over. Traffic was moving slowly. I was afraid of being late, and as I drove, I began to cry. I was tired, not just physically—though that was definitely true—but at the core of my being. *Why am I doing this?* I asked myself repeatedly.

Why am I even here in L.A.? For that matter, why am I even alive? The questions rolled through my mind as the tears rolled down my cheeks.

It all seems so hopeless. I'm not strong enough to be doing this—that much is clear. I'm not getting the consistent work I need for a steady income. I'm rarely happy. I never have enough money but I don't have any more hours in the day to spare for making more money. Maybe it's time to leave L.A., I thought. *I've tried this long enough. It's time to give up.*

On acting? On life? Maybe.

This wasn't the dream life I had come here to live. I had the bleached blonde hair with extensions, the fake tanning-bed tan, and the eating disorder to prove it. And yet, no matter how hard I worked, how much I sold of myself, I never could get my big break. Friendships were shallow; men were proving to be takers far more than givers; and significant acting jobs were being given out left and right—just never to me.

But I knew those weren't my only problems, or even the main ones. My personal life—body and soul—was deeply broken.

The sun was just starting to set as I drove toward the church. The light at La Brea and Sunset turned the same yellow as the sky, and I braked as it went red. I put my head in my hands and began to sob. "Are you real, God? Then show me!" I cried out, "Are you even out there? Show me, because I have no will to live. I am done." I wept there at that stoplight as the weight of the day and this dream and all the rejections fell hard on my shoulders.

At that stoplight, I'd finally reached the point of falling apart.

I was broken in ways I cannot explain. My history came rushing back, and all the times I had failed, all the times I had been failed by others, flooded me with sorrows too deep for words. I just didn't want to do this anymore. This journey. This story. This life.

The tears wouldn't stop. To say it was my lowest point, the rock-bottom moment, seems cliché, but it is how I felt and still feel about that day. I cried and cried right there at that stoplight where La Brea hits Sunset. And it was a long light.

A horn honked—but it wasn't behind me. The light was still red, so I knew no one was telling me to go. It was alongside me, in the lane to my left. I was embarrassed by my tears (always the perfectionist, worried even about what complete strangers would think) and didn't want to look over there, so I just kept my head down, but the honking continued. Again. Again. Again.

Finally I looked up. In a beat-up red car, an older Hispanic man sat in the driver's seat, holding up a white piece of paper. Across it, scribbled and traced over and over in pen, it read, "99.5 FM." He pointed to the radio and then to his sign, and he kept pointing his finger back and forth between the two while nodding to me expectantly.

I couldn't imagine why he was doing this.

As the light turned green, he drove away with a small wave, and I noticed his bumper sticker: JESUS LOVES YOU. As I drove through the intersection, I pressed the radio's search button until it reached 99.5 FM.

"If you are hopeless and at the end of your rope, God loves you and has a plan for your life," a man's voice boomed through the speakers. He was answering the very question I had just cried out to God! "God is real. And he is with you."

No way. No way did that pastor on the radio respond directly to the very thing I had just cried out. I could not believe it. My mouth hung open as I drove, listening to the voice on the radio tell me over and over that God was real and was with me.

An immense flood of relief poured over me.

I knew deep within me in that very moment that God actually *is* real. I was shocked, to be sure, but deeply comforted. For all my years of handling life as if no one greater than me existed and could control the situation, suddenly I knew.

I knew that God is real.

My heart pounded. I felt goose bumps rise on my arms and down the back of my neck. My tears slowed. My ache turned to relief.

God is real. There was no way this was a coincidence. I had cried out for him to reveal himself, and seconds later, a total stranger was scribbling down and waving the call letters of a station that was sharing God's answer to my prayer—the voice of a pastor repeating the words I had just cried out to God.

With a sense of wonder, I kept driving toward the church. I pulled into the parking lot, dried my tears, fixed my smudged makeup, walked into the coaching session as if I were already a star, and did my best to soak in all I could from this not inexpensive one-on-one session with Christina Hart. But it all felt like a dream. My heart was still in my car, pondering how a kind man motioned for me to turn on my radio and reliving what seemed like nothing less than a miracle.

God had reached down from the heavens and touched me.

I didn't tell anyone about that moment at the stoplight, the red car, the hand-scribbled sign, or the preacher on the radio. I couldn't have found the words if I'd tried. And I couldn't bear to have the moment soiled by someone else's doubt or disbelief, for the moment was the single purest moment of my life up to that point. It never left my mind. Where I had been hopeless at that intersection, I was now hopeful. My situation didn't change; my pockets didn't fill with cash; my phone didn't ring off the hook with opportunities in Hollywood—but I was different. I was changed. I was convinced there was a God.

I didn't know how I was changed or what it all meant.

I only knew that my story, with so many chapters already lived, now felt like it was just beginning.

CHANGING DIRECTION

A sense of mystery seemed to blanket the following weeks. I kept my normal routine, going through all the same motions that had marked my life for what seemed like forever, yet I had a profound sense that my entire life had just changed. I simply didn't know how yet. It was otherworldly. Mysterious.

My memories of the spiritual weight-loss program that I had shoved aside in the distractions of my life reemerged front and center. At home in my bedroom, out of Jenni's view, I opened my Bible for the first time in months and began to read. I didn't know where to begin or what it all meant, but this time, I knew I wasn't holding some ancient self-help manual—I was holding the story of a true and living God.

And I prayed. I wept and asked God to show me more of himself. I'm not sure what I was expecting, but I was puzzled when it seemed that nothing happened. I found myself revisiting old memories—good and bad. My brother and cousins calling me names, Mattie's mom praying over their meals, my after-school loneliness eating sweets in front of the TV. I thought of my parents' divorce, my hours of writing poems to my father a thousand miles away, the searing burn of my shame at my mother's choices—it was as if in revisiting my story, I hoped God would speak to me about it.

Abandonment. Self-destructive thoughts and choices. Anger, resentment, and the push toward self-sufficiency that arose out of it—where had God been through all of that? I had no idea. But I couldn't shake the feeling that a turning point had come and it was time for me to make a change, to shift direction. I knew that this past year, while living at Jenni's, I'd gone from bad to worse. Blake, Joe, Scott, and my partying life weren't fulfilling at all. Hollywood and its elusive promise of success continued to wear me down. My finances had certainly gone from poor to miserably hopeless.

I spoke to no one about my dramatic encounter at the stoplight with the living God, but I could not shake my certainty that this was too important to ignore. I *had* to change direction.

But how? Where?

Chapter 11

BABY CHRISTIAN

> My goal is that they may be encouraged in heart and
> united in love, so that they may have the full riches of
> complete understanding, in order that they may know the
> mystery of God, namely, Christ, in whom are hidden all
> the treasures of wisdom and knowledge.
>
> COLOSSIANS 2:2–3

"Andrea, do you know of a good church where Mike could go? I think
he really needs God in his life."

I was taken aback by the question from Mike's mom.

(It's fascinating to look back now and see the series of events that
God folded into the wake of my decision to invite him into my life. One
God-thing after another. All gifts from heaven, though I didn't recognize
such things yet.)

It was a January weekend in 2001, and I'd joined my friend Mike
for a meal at his apartment while his mom was in town. Since his mom
was talking about getting him to church, I figured he must have told her
about his problem with pot. For most of the people in my circle, smoking
pot wasn't seen as a problem at all. If your substance abuse was under
control enough that you could drag yourself out of bed and get to work
to keep from losing your job, you were good. But Mike's parents didn't

see it that way. For him, it *was* a problem, and though he continued to use it anyway, he was struggling to stop.

Mike had left for a minute to take out the garbage when his mom popped the church question. I almost laughed at first, wondering why she would think I would know of a church. I hadn't told anyone of my God experience at the stoplight. What would make her think I would know of a church? (Maybe I was a pretty innocent-looking girl—at least to a mom!)

I had only ever been to one church in the area: Malibu Vineyard, compliments of Hef's limo, and that felt like ages ago. Even though I'd been reading the Bible since the stoplight incident, I hadn't been interested in going to a church. I wasn't looking to get caught up in practicing a religion—I just wanted a personal connection with God, something private and powerful and real, like my mysterious encounter with him at the intersection. My impression of church people was that they were into religion and religious practices, rules, and long lists of don'ts. That didn't appeal to me at all. Church people were different from me, and I didn't want to be like them.

But I was happy to tell her I'd do what I could to get Mike to church. How ironic! *I was going to go to church for Mike because* he *needed it*, I thought, *not me!* I didn't have the slightest inkling that Malibu Vineyard was about to play a major part in the complete transformation of my life. But God did. He knew this little church was where, after years of heading resolutely down the wrong path, I would step onto the narrow path that led upward toward spiritual health rather than the path toward spiritual death.

A week or so passed until one Sunday morning, Mike and I were on our way to Malibu Vineyard Church. I don't remember what we talked about on our way. I only remember that as I drove the same final few blocks that I'd traveled in Hef's limo three years before, I wasn't talking about hair extensions and manicures. I was wondering, even hesitantly anticipating, if this church experience might be different for me than it was that first time. *Would I feel God or hear him like I had that day in the car?* I hoped so.

I led us straight to the center row, center seats, figuring that if God was going to show up, I wanted the best seats in the house.

From the moment the service began, I sensed something new, something fresh, happening. A Presence wrapped itself around me. Clean. Different. I'd been living my life surrounded by things that made me feel dirty for so long, but as the people sang, something resonated deep within, urging that I tune in to everything happening around me. As I did, the Presence grew, and before long, I knew I was enveloped in pure love. P-U-R-E. I wanted it. I wanted more of it. I wanted it to infuse me and chase out all the darkness I had carried inside me for so long.

Then the pastor spoke. He was from South Africa, and his fascinating accent held me as mesmerized by the sound of his words as by his message. Even though I didn't understand what I was feeling, what it all meant, or how it was happening, I was so deeply moved by his words that when he ended the sermon, I ached for more. So much so, that at the end of the service when the pastor said, "If you want Jesus to be Lord of your life, raise your hand," I instantly raised mine, and so did Mike! "Now close your eyes," the pastor said, "and confess your sins to God. And tell him that you accept Jesus as your Savior."

And I did. I said the words. And I meant them with my entire being.

If I were to choose a *moment* that I declared I was "saved," this would be it. My experience at the stoplight had shown me that God was real. But on this day, I made a choice to invite God's pure presence to invade me, to change me, and to wash away all the dirt and shadows I had carried with me all my life. God had led me to that choice by revealing in the months prior that I'd made my pain even worse in the past three years. Now I wanted all that filth replaced with his purity and light.

That January 2001 day was the intentional decision that began my transformation from a dating-around, drug-experimenting, celebrity-partying, morally challenged woman into the follower of Christ I am today—"perfectly unfinished" though I still am.

Began is the key word here. Everything about me did not change at that instant, nor did I quickly gain a complete understanding of what God wanted in my life or how to get there. But I did know that day that God, the one true God, wasn't just "out there somewhere." He was now a part of my life. I left there knowing I wanted more of him. I was desperate for more. I was like a child, wanting to be wherever God was, to feel his presence again and again.

So week after week, I went back to the church, where I eagerly anticipated what God would say to me through the music, the worship, and the pastor's messages. I wondered how this faith stuff was going to change my life. But that was okay with me. I *wanted* change—God-change. I had a hunger to feel God's presence. I wanted to talk with him and to hear his words. I had tons of questions, and Sunday after Sunday, I felt like I was experiencing something new about God and his love for me.

My honeymoon with Jesus had begun.

BABY STEPS

One evening while praying, I considered my recent bright spots. I had earned my certification as a personal trainer, and though I hadn't yet figured out how to make a living at it, it had given me a new skill set and positive growth that felt deeply satisfying. I'd made a few new friends at Crunch Fitness, even a few guys I knew I wouldn't get romantically involved with. How great to enjoy friendships that didn't revolve around parties, drinking, and sex! And with that realization, I knew I didn't *want* to fit into my current friends' social circle anymore. I needed to steer clear of the parties my current friendships had brought into my life. Besides, I had to face the fact that I couldn't pay such high rent and still cover utilities, car, insurance, and groceries, much less acting lessons. I decided I needed to move out of Jenni's place.

But how could I make my exit? The thought of conflict with Jenni set my stomach churning. On the one hand, she wouldn't be happy to suddenly lose my share of the rent. On the other hand, she had never been hurting for money. I knew she could easily get by until she found a new roommate, and knowing Jenni—the beautiful, bubbly extrovert—she'd fill that spot in a heartbeat.

Once I'd made my decision to move out, a sense of urgency took over. I wanted out now. I wanted off the party train and out of drowning in the shame of struggling and not being able to pay rent. Without telling Jenni, I rented a storage unit, made plans to move my few belongings when she'd be at work, and pulled it off within a few days. I knew it was cowardly to slip a note under her bedroom door, but that's what I did, simply explaining the truth—that I couldn't afford the rent anymore and had to move—and thanking her for everything.

Mike offered his place while he was in rehab, and I knew I was overworked and weary of the ceaseless scrambling to pay my bills. I took him up on his kind offer. He entered rehab, and I moved onto the floor of the little office loft he had in his apartment.

Now comes the evidence that I was a brand-new Christian still learning what it meant. I was still working at the sushi restaurant in Westwood where I had met Joe Francis. Occasionally, Joe would ask me out, and I'd say yes. Scott and I were still dating occasionally, and the fact that Joe and Scott didn't know about each other—*Well, no big deal*, I told myself. After all, we weren't in a committed relationship. I was a free agent. And after my dates, I came home to sleep on the floor of Mike's loft.

When Mike completed his stint in rehab and came home, I continued staying on the floor in his loft. Our relationship had never been a romance, but always a friendship. Right? I was about to discover it was not that way for Mike. Within a few weeks of his return home, I realized he was angry. He couldn't bear to see me being picked up in Joe's Ferrari for a date—something he made crystal clear the next morning.

"Look, Andrea. I've been in love with you since before you moved in, and clearly you don't feel the same way—you're still dating other guys. This is just too hard for me. You've got to move out."

I understood. I'd never meant to hurt Mike. I had always been perfectly clear that I saw us as friends, nothing more. I hadn't been aware of his hurt until that very moment, and I felt awful. I promised I'd be out in a hurry.

On that same day, I was scheduled to do some administrative work for Scott, so I headed to his home office. Scott greeted me with surprising news: a wealthy prince in Dubai had requested that Scott be his personal trainer.

"I was wondering if you'd like to house-sit for me for a few months," he said. "You can keep my office running smoothly while you keep an eye on my place."

This was bizarre—and perfect. Coincidental timing? Or God's hand at work?

I accepted the offer and moved in that very night.

THE PRESSURE LIFTS

Now that I was no longer trying to keep up with friends and the social whirlwind of parties, I focused on building my clientele at Crunch Fitness, waitressing at the sushi place, going to acting classes, and keeping my ear to the ground for word of auditions.

I continued to date Joe casually when he was in town. But with Scott in Dubai, I didn't have to do any balancing acts or keep secrets. That relieved some pressure. Blake, on the other hand, like a bad penny, just kept turning up, hanging out during my shifts to drink and flirt. I was proud of myself for maintaining my distance. He finally got the message.

One day in Beverly Hills, I ran into Austin, a regular customer I knew from the sushi restaurant—yet another man who wanted more than friendship. The two of us had often chatted about life's struggles and disappointments. But now he was filled with an optimism I'd never seen in him before, and he couldn't stop raving about a conference he had just attended. "Andrea, it changed my life. Really. It's a weeklong conference on personal growth and development. I'll never be the same. You oughta go!" I was intrigued, especially in light of my newfound belief in God. Maybe this would be a step in the right direction. A few weeks went by, and every time I saw him, he urged me to go to the conference.

"Austin, I can't afford a one-week conference," I told him one day.

"I'll pay for you to go, Andrea. I really want to pass this on to others."

Touched and curious, I put in for some time off and registered. The conference was fascinating. It stressed growing and changing, making amends with people, and restoring relationships. That very week, I reached out with an apology to Jenni and Mike by writing letters, and I also called Dad and his girlfriend, Pat, in a heartfelt attempt to build new bridges in our relationship.

But something kept gnawing at me. The conference offered lots of positive techniques and principles, but it was all about self—self-help, self-actualization, self-fulfillment. I had tried so many self-help avenues in the past, all with the same result. Now came a huge realization that it was that very "self" that had brought me to the end of my rope. I hadn't come to this conference hoping to find more self-fix-it secrets; I'd come looking for more—something *beyond self.* After the last session on the last day of the event, I got into my car and sat quietly, reviewing the conference materials.

In a rush of realization, I knew I didn't want or need more of *self;* I wanted and needed more of *God.* And to my surprise, I was genuinely disappointed that I hadn't discovered anything about God—and I had really hoped to do so. I still didn't know what it meant, but I knew it wasn't this. (I hadn't caught on yet that the revelation about where my "self" had led me *was* God's lesson!) I tossed the materials into the backseat and headed home to Scott's place.

As the next month passed with Scott in Dubai, I realized that there was no question I was having the most peaceful months I'd had in a very long time. Not that my health had improved or my food issues had diminished, or that my work, acting classes, and audition schedules let up, but I felt a pressure lift. No doubt, removing the pressure of paying rent I couldn't afford helped a lot. But it was more than that. I was spending some time again reading the Bible, and my sense of awe at the mystery of how God showed himself so miraculously to me at the stoplight stayed with me.

It wasn't long before that honeymoon period was put to a test. Scott returned home from Dubai. I decided not to tell him about my spiritual adventures. I sensed he'd dismiss it, and I knew that would hurt me. Instead of declaring that I had changed, I acted as if nothing had changed at all. He didn't ask me to move out when he returned, and I didn't offer to, so for about a month, we lived together as a couple. Then one evening, Scott explained that he had no interest in having a girlfriend live with him. He preferred living alone. I was fine with that. We both agreed we weren't interested in an exclusive or committed relationship.

The next day, while working my shift at the sushi restaurant, I spread the word among friends that I was looking for a roommate. I heard that a friend of a friend, Nancy, was also looking for a roommate. She and I met up at a restaurant in Santa Monica.

Nancy was a gem, a Catholic who loved the Lord. I moved in with her in a nice place in Brentwood near the beach. I was just turning twenty-three, and she was forty. It wasn't long before I considered her like an older sister I'd never had. She was very genuine and caring. (She would one day be in my wedding.)

While Nancy was a wonderful plus factor in my life, I still clung to the familiar relationships with Joe and Scott that I still thought of as positive. One evening, Scott and I went out on a date and were intimate with one another. To my surprise, my heart was crushed with a feeling of sadness. I simply knew that what I'd done was wrong—that my action grieved God. These were the birth pangs of my emerging conscience. I became aware that my conscience knew right from wrong, and because I was really trying to love God, I felt sad. I tried to compensate by taking Scott to church with me. One time was all it took! He made it clear he was neither comfortable nor interested, and it became clear during the service that I couldn't have both God and Scott. I also knew I needed God more than I needed Scott, which meant there was no room for Scott.

Clearly, my moral compass was being recalibrated by the Holy Spirit.

My job at Crunch Fitness as a personal trainer was beginning to pay off as my clientele list grew. Even so, I was still waitressing, and my finances, as usual, were stretched thin. Having begun to grasp the importance of taking my needs to God, my finances became a prayer request. Soon I concluded that waitressing was not going to help me achieve my goals, so I invested more time and energy in building my fitness clientele and cut down on waitressing—before finally quitting it entirely.

Since Crunch was in Hollywood, a lot of celebrities worked out there. One of my clients, Paddy Cullen, was a successful producer. As we worked together, I'd tell her of my dreams and efforts to pursue acting. She kindly offered to help me get my Screen Actor's Guild (SAG) card, an absolute necessity if you wanted to be an actor in Hollywood on union shows. Her offer was a tremendous help and encouragement, as the process is arduous.

Crunch Fitness was being used by God for my benefit in more ways than just the money. How could I have not been aware of how many clients and other personal trainers were Christians? Some even attended Malibu Vineyard. One day during my own workout, I began talking with a woman next to me—Christine. Our conversation quickly turned to faith, and soon we were laughing at the discovery that we both went to the Vineyard. We agreed to meet after the service later that week and grab lunch—a tradition we continued for several years. Christine is still one of my dearest friends to this day—such a close friend that she was my maid of honor in my wedding.

One day I happened to mention to Christine that Scott and I would see each other once in a while. "Are you sleeping with him?" she asked.

I nodded, explaining my experience of guilt, yet confessing I'd done so a few times since.

"*What!* What are you thinking? Andrea, you're a Christian now," she said. "Don't you know what God says? You can't sleep with him. Or anybody else you're not married to."

I warned you—I was only a baby Christian. I was just beginning to learn what the Bible taught about our hearts, bodies, and behavior, and the deep connection between those three. Had my conscience at times told me the things I'd been doing for the past few years were wrong? Of course. But I'd never had any guidelines in my life to let me know what was truly right or wrong when it came to sexuality. My new Christian friends, even new believers like Christine, were not only becoming cheerleaders encouraging me on in this new life, but they were also helping me learn how to use my moral compass, the compass set to God as True North. They helped me see my mistakes and directed me back to the right path.

Don't think for a moment that this was a smooth or consistent process—a steady path in the right direction. The truth is, I bucked against it at least as often as I accepted it. I felt a great tension between my hunger for this new, righteous way of life and the fun and familiarity of the old one. For instance, despite Christine's blunt comments, I didn't immediately break things off with Scott—or with Joe, for that matter. I still hadn't found my voice or the conviction to say the hard things.

NEW CHOICES ALL AROUND

Christine and I continued to go to church together, but now I began sitting in a different place from her. Christine was a front-row person, and though I tried that a few times, I quickly realized how uncomfortable

I was. I gravitated to the back of the church, usually in the very last row. The act of worship had become something profoundly intimate between Jesus and me—so sweet and precious that I didn't want anyone, not even Christine, to be a part of it. I didn't want to socialize with others afterward, and I didn't want anyone watching me. I wanted to be able to close my eyes, raise and lower my hands, lift my face toward heaven or lower it in humble reverence. This experience was private, and sitting in the last row near the exit allowed me to become as invisible as possible.

Through worship and the preaching of God's word, I was learning more every week about God and his holiness and purity. As I did, the Holy Spirit worked increasingly on my heart. I was hungry for more of Jesus. But the more I knew him, the more I was becoming aware of the sin inside of me. I didn't yet grasp that God loves me unconditionally. I didn't know the difference between guilt and shame: that healthy guilt is a conviction that our actions are wrong and need to be corrected, but that shame is a weapon the enemy uses to go far beyond wrong actions and tell us we are worthless and have no value. And as for *grace*—the completely unmerited, undeserved gift of God's blessing and forgiveness—it wasn't even on my radar yet.

I had a battle going on inside me, yet—if this makes any sense at all—it was a profoundly sweet battle. God was goodness. I wanted and was finding more of that. God was love, and I was just beginning to understand the truth that love—real love—was far more than a feeling. But where did God's love and my choices and behaviors and God's desires for me all meet? Of that I wasn't sure.

On the one hand, my life was taking on a new shape. Christine and I got involved in Bible studies and small groups. And the Christians at Crunch Fitness encouraged me and loved on me. On the other hand, being desired and pursued by men had for quite some time been my way of meeting my lifelong desire to belong, and it had helped quiet the voices in my head that said I wasn't enough. As I grew in my faith, though,

I knew I couldn't have both, at least not in the way I was handling my relationships with men. So I made what was for me an incredibly difficult decision. I decided to be obedient to Christ. To give up control in my relationships, let Jesus tell me what to do, and then respond by doing it.

This was huge for me.

As soon as I made that decision, I was tested. Joe called and said, "Let's go out on Friday."

I said, "You know, Joe, I'm a Christian now."

"And sooooo?"

I said, "If we go out, you're going to expect me to sleep with you. And I don't do that now. I'm different."

"Well, we'll see." His smug tone of voice told me he wasn't convinced I meant it. He was sure he could change my mind; that the "old magic" would return once the two of us were out together.

We did go out. At the end of the evening, I said good night with a modest kiss. I can still remember the surprised look on his face as I closed the door. We dated a few times after that, with the same ending. And something truly beautiful happened along the way. Remember those old labels from my childhood? The crybaby and fraidycat who was too weak to stand up for herself (and who got run over by an ATV as a result); the self-sufficient teenager who so longed to belong that she did drugs and shoplifted because that's what cool kids did; the conflict avoider who just slipped away without bringing closure with David Spade, Jenni, and Mike. Something mysterious was happening. Those old labels were beginning to fade and loosen their grip on my life. Honestly, I don't know who was more surprised when I made it clear to Joe that no meant no—Joe or me!

A Bible verse I'd heard at church suddenly became real to me: "Therefore, if anyone is in Christ, the new creation has come: The old has gone, the new is here!" (2 Corinthians 5:17).

The old me really *was* gone, and the new me—someone with a growing boldness and an emerging sensitivity to the Holy Spirit—was looking back at me in the mirror. I was a new creation.

The child I had been had felt ashamed of the things my mother did—as if my value and worth were damaged by her behavior. That old shame of being defined by my family's choices was beginning to fade. I was a child of the living God.

The teenager I had been, and the woman I'd been until being saved, had felt no guilt for my own choices and behaviors. But that was changing as well. I had a new identity in Christ. And with that came a new kind of guilt over my actions—not an identity-crushing shame, but rather a nudging and prodding to clean up my own act. I was beginning to see things in an entirely new way. New thoughts, new ideas, new motivations. Something new was at work inside me—new life. Something completely alien to the way I had always lived. Alien, yet welcomed.

Who would have thought that saying no to a guy would bring such excitement?

Who else but God? God knew that the more I practiced obedience to him, the greater my passion would grow for living as he wanted me to live.

Through my decision to let Christ be in control over my relationship with Joe, I discovered something I needed to clearly understand. What had kept him attracted all that time was not who I was on the inside, but rather what he could get from me. Our relationship had never been about me; it had always been about Joe and his desires. God wasn't a cosmic killjoy. His standards of behavior were there for *my good* and *my protection*. This was a brand-new concept to me. Now that I was discovering what it means to be born again, I vowed to save myself, from that moment forward, for my future husband. For the most part, I just felt like I was done with guys for a while. I decided I didn't trust my instincts about men as much as I used to. Those instincts hadn't served me well.

SPIRITUAL FIRE

More and more, I was on fire for the Lord. I began waking up at five o'clock in the morning just to turn on Joyce Meyer's TV show, *Enjoying Everyday Life*, to hear God's Word and love taught. To this day, I love her—she's still one of my favorite pastors. I looked forward to praying and spending time in the Bible. I didn't always understand what I was reading in the Bible, but I was there, ready for God to speak to my heart.

The Vineyard was known as a charismatic church—which means the Holy Spirit and spiritual gifts are an active part of the worship experience, and so the Spirit became an active and crucial part of my own worship. My prayer language brought me the closest I could imagine to the presence of God—even closer than when I was new to the church, sitting up front and center.

One weekend, Christine and I went to a retreat at Lake Arrowhead, and we were slain in the Holy Spirit. It's hard to describe if you haven't experienced or witnessed it. To some observers, it may have looked like we fainted. But the experience for me was like floating down in the power of God, surrounded by the beauty and purity and peace of his strength. It was an incredible, life-changing experience, feeding me with spiritual fire at the deepest level of my soul.

Each step, each month, God was amping up his perfecting work. And he was about to bring a completely unexpected, life-changing blessing into my life.

Chapter 12

THE *FEAR FACTOR* SURVIVOR

The Sovereign LORD is my strength;
he makes my feet like the feet of a deer,
he enables me to tread on the heights.

HABAKKUK 3:19

David A. R. White and his friend Jeff were attending Malibu Vineyard in June 2001 when they saw a girl with long, blonde, dread-like braids, arms raised, worshiping Jesus in the back row of the church.

Yup. That would be me.

Remember, I chose the back row specifically so I wouldn't be seen and wouldn't need to interact with others. I was totally into worship and thankfully was oblivious that I was being observed—and that my unselfconscious communion with God had captured the heart of the man who would one day become my husband.

As for my dreads, they were funky, free-falling, and fun, and thus seemed a perfect match for the free-spirited woman I felt myself becoming. I was totally immersed in my new liberty from the guilt and shame of the old lifestyle. I was done living by standards that I had slid into rather than aspired to. Being myself was a new life skill for me, and my abandonment to worship and praise was feeding my strength to be myself in Christ. I suspect, looking back, that my blonde dreads reflected the boldness that had risen in me to be fully myself and to set out to define myself in Christ rather than by any preconceived molds of what others expected me to be or even what I expected myself to be.

So the year 2001 became the year of the new me. New self, new lifestyle, new way of relating to others and the world. From the moment in January when I raised my hand in church to accept Jesus, things began to change drastically. Over the months, knowing, loving, and sharing Jesus became my number-one priority. I wanted to give nothing less than an all-out, 100 percent effort for God. Radical for Jesus. I had never felt so free in my life.

Who would have imagined those dreads would usher a love story into my life by catching the eye of one David A. R. White?

Not that I was looking for a man in my life. I wasn't! I was on my honeymoon with Jesus. I didn't need—didn't *want*—a man in my life. I'd made too many bad choices, and for now, I was *so* over men. Jesus had flooded my heart with more love than I had ever imagined, and I figured I didn't have any room left over for a man.

David, of course, didn't know that. After church, he and Jeff came over to introduce themselves. Honestly, I was fairly detached and didn't show much interest, since I didn't want to encourage them.

They didn't give up. A few weeks later, they found me after the service and invited me to pizza at Jeff's house. Christine was with me, and they invited her along with other people, so it seemed to be a safe enough invitation. David and I had a pleasant conversation, but he was just one among several with whom I chatted, and I purposely kept it brief.

The following week, I spotted them looking for me and dodged out a side door. Over the next few months, I managed to avoid them by attending early service, sitting in the back, and bolting out the door before church was over. I didn't want any romantic involvement whatsoever, not even a hint of it, as if I intuitively knew I needed time to let my heart recalibrate. No doubt the Holy Spirit was at work in me.

One Sunday, though, I attended the later service. I must have been less vigilant, because David caught up with me. In fact, I had the distinct impression he'd been lying in wait for me. "Hey," he said, "we're all going out to lunch. Want to come?"

"Sorry. I can't. But Julie is available," I said, referring to a friend at church. "Why don't you ask her?"

As I turned to walk away, I caught sight of David looking completely baffled. I guess he thought I was telling him to *date* her, when I was only suggesting someone who might enjoy going to lunch with his group—someone, anyone, who was *not* me.

Shortly afterward, David and Jeff stopped attending Malibu Vineyard and began going to Bel Air Presbyterian. Maybe they would find the wives they were looking for there. Whew! That was the end of that.

Or so I thought.

AN INVITATION TO *SURVIVOR*

In contrast to dodging David and romance in general, I was embracing the adventures God brought my way. The more I grew in my faith, the more I began to understand how faith spilled into every aspect of my life, including my job. As a trainer, I was used to encouraging people to push beyond their limits to grow stronger in body. And of course, that meant taking my own advice, working hard to keep my body in shape. After all, a trainer's body is the best advertisement for how good of a trainer he or she is.

Now I was seeing that not only could I push myself to take steps to grow my faith through dedicating time and energy to worship, Bible study, and prayer, but I could also be an influence on others simply by encouraging people to think about their own spiritual well-being. And the best way to do it was by sharing my own. I loved finding casual and friendly ways to talk about my faith adventure as part of my everyday life. It was freeing to think of sharing my faith not so much as a "task" of evangelism (which sounded so daunting), but rather as a natural overflow of simply being my real self and sharing what mattered to me with the people I encountered every day.

The atmosphere at Crunch Fitness was a friendly one. Trainers knew most of the clients, and the regular clients came to know most of the trainers, at least well enough to say hello and sometimes have a longer chat about something—whether of consequence or not. A number of entertainment industry people were Crunch clients, and we treated them with the same open friendliness offered to everyone who came through our doors. Tyler, a producer of the TV show *Survivor*, was one of them. I knew him well enough to say hello.

In the fall of 2001, *Survivor* was ramping up for its fifth season. I enjoyed the show, and as a trainer, I respected the contestants as they pushed hard in difficult circumstances—not only to survive, but to challenge themselves to overcome obstacles beyond their known limits and far beyond what most people could do.

Tyler was always looking for intriguing contestants, and one day he approached me and asked, "Would you ever want to be on the show *Survivor*?"

I thought he was joking. When I realized he was serious, I couldn't believe it. Back then, *Survivor* was *the* reality show, the cream of the crop in the reality-show world. I felt a surge of excitement. Here it was—the ultimate challenge for my body and spirit. Even better than that, wow, just think of all the people I could reach for Jesus! Not just the contestants, but also the filming crew, the producers, and the television audience. And who knew what doors God might open after that? But mostly the idea of being able to share my faith—perhaps all over the world—made me giddy with excitement.

Why me? I'm guessing that since I was a personal trainer, Tyler figured I'd be in decent condition and able to compete well. Plus, my blonde dreadlocks made me stand out a bit—a positive on a show that wanted its characters to be unique and memorable.

When he explained the rigorous selection process, I realized that if I made it to the final rounds of those approved for the cast, financially this would be a significant challenge. I would have to take two weeks off—without pay—to be a part of the arduous final selection process in which they narrowed the final twenty-five participants down to the chosen sixteen. The finances would be a huge deal for me, because though I'd been supporting myself since coming to L.A., I was still just scraping by. Even so, I eagerly agreed.

I had a blast sailing through all the initial selection steps and soon found myself in the final twenty-five. Because *Survivor* takes such a toll on the participants, the producers want to be sure its contestants can handle the psychological, physical, and emotional demands of the show. To do this, they put us in seclusion at a Doubletree Hotel. For about two weeks, we had no TV, no phones, no computers, no outside contact with the world whatsoever. We couldn't hang out with the other applicants. We even had to eat by ourselves, and we were allowed to talk with only the staff.

The producers interviewed us a number of times and in a number of ways throughout the two weeks to make sure we wouldn't have a breakdown in the middle of the show and to see how we would do under stress with no one to rely on but ourselves. We also had physicals, psychological evaluations, and weight checks. I weighed in at 105 pounds, and after my physical, they told me, "If you're selected, we want you to gain ten pounds before we start shooting."

I remained super excited throughout the two weeks of seclusion. Determined to gain the weight, I made a point of eating healthy snacks— and lots of them. And still enthralled with Jesus during this honeymoon time of my faith, I welcomed this time alone as a spiritual retreat, so I spent my time in the hotel reading my Bible, praying, journaling, and being joyful in the Spirit. Having studied previous seasons of the show, I realized that contestants with unique personalities were the ones who stood out. *Well, I guess I'll be the Jesus chick*, I decided. That way, I'd be myself and make the most of every opportunity to share my faith boldly as often as I could, on camera and off.

At the end of the two weeks, we were able to go home. Would I make it into the final sixteen? Confident I had done all I could, I was grateful that I didn't feel anxious or desperate to be chosen. I was spiritually confident that God's will would be done, and I could rest in that. I did not receive a call to be a contestant, and though I felt some disappointment, I was wonderfully grateful for the experience I'd had.

At church the following Sunday, a friend who had a friend on the *Survivor* crew sought me out. "I know why they didn't pick you," she said. "They all thought you would have done great, but they just felt you were a bit too Jesusy for the show—a little too bold with your faith. Otherwise, they loved you!"

I was too bold in Jesus for the show? That was a reason I could live with! After all, I'd simply been myself in that regard. Though I was disappointed, I'd been so sure this was an opportunity from God, and I saw it as a wonderful lesson that God is not predictable. He had opened the door to audition, but he gave no guarantee that he'd open the door for me to be on the show. I needed to trust that he had accomplished what he wanted to accomplish in that time (whether in me or in others), and to release my expectations of anything more. God was trustworthy, even when he surprised me—a lesson he would soon reinforce in other areas of my life.

A few months later, I was chatting with Tyler at Crunch. He mentioned how much they had liked me during the *Survivor* tryouts, and then he said, "You know, I'd like to put you on something else. I'm thinking *Fear Factor*. Would you be interested?"

I hesitated. Let me tell you, *Fear Factor* was not quite in the same category of highly respected reality shows as *Survivor*.

At first I wasn't going to do it. Would I be embarrassed to tell my friends I was on the show? After nearly making it onto *Survivor*, this felt like a compromise. But then I looked at it differently. God seemed to be opening another door. Would I step through it? Ever since I was a little girl, I'd been wired to be a competitor. Athletic. But I'd also been the little girl who was told by her brothers that I couldn't go in the house until I threw like a boy. I had responded by becoming a great thrower, and ever since, I liked to challenge myself, competing against myself and others. To go to the limits of what I had done before and then try to beat it. So what if I flamed out magnificently, like in the trampoline fiasco as a child where I broke my glasses? At least I would try. Just as I might not have been the best volleyball player on the team as a kid, I was still one of the hardest-working players. That's how I got better.

Besides, this was a chance for the scrawny little girl still inside me who got picked on by my brother and cousins to prove myself. So the competitor in me won. I decided to go for it.

NEW FACTORS

Now, years later, in the writing of this book, I can see that something else came into play. It's as if moving from *Survivor* to *Fear Factor* provided an unexpected metaphor for this major transition time in my life. Giving my heart to Jesus had ignited the fighter in me in a very positive way. I was coming to realize that though I'd been victimized several times by others in my life, God had grown me into a survivor. I began to see that he had used all my past experiences for my benefit and growth. No matter what life had thrown at me, no matter how hard my enemy had tried to destroy, dismantle, derail, or distract me, God had seen to it that I would find a way to get back up and keep moving forward.

Had I made some major mistakes along the way? And some really poor choices? Absolutely! But now I could appreciate that when my mother went to live elsewhere, I didn't give up. I put myself in the place of the absent parents and took care of my little brother and myself the best I could, emotionally and physically. I did what I needed to do to put one foot in front of the other, to move ahead, to survive. There were times when it was much easier than other times.

Then, throughout my season of association with the Playboy Mansion, having stepped into the flowing river of celebrities, aspiring actors, and powerful people, I had convinced myself that I needed to fight to become an actor in the way others had—taking on flexible jobs like waitressing and the bikini bar to put food on the table and allow me time for acting classes and auditions. I'd moved from a survivor to a fighter, but my fight had been all about me—my becoming an actor and fulfilling my dreams. I had chosen to go with the flow and swim in their river, but I discovered the hard way that all the swimming in the world wasn't getting me to my destination. Instead, despite fighting my way toward success, I'd been drowning.

But then Jesus came along and plucked me out of that river, dried me off, and set me on solid ground. Instead of my churning legs only finding water underneath me and being powerless against the current, I was now running for a new goal—to try to get it right with God. I was straining forward on an exciting new path of a personal relationship with God, straining to "get" this relationship with Jesus that was wonderfully mysterious. That was something worth fighting for.

I realized that I wanted to do *Fear Factor*. I wanted to face my fears head-on. I wanted to grow stronger in every way and be used by God any way he saw fit. I wanted to challenge myself to tackle whatever God put in front of me and do it well.

And the fact that there was a $50,000 prize for winning was not a downside.

Again, we were put up in a hotel. Nothing ritzy. Just a basic hotel in North Hollywood. In fact, how ironic to discover it was just off Vineland

Avenue, at the very exit I used when I lived with Sarah and Olivia. While the machinery for *Survivor* had moved at a slower pace, *Fear Factor* was on a fast track. Within weeks, with cameras rolling, I was standing at the foot of the beautiful historic bridge in Pasadena (nicknamed "Suicide Bridge" for a reason) with five other contestants—three guys and two women. By then, I'd shed my dreadlocks for my "normal" hairstyle—long and straight. I was the smallest person in the group and therefore teased as the one most likely to fail. Shadows of childhood all over again!

One of my greatest life fears is that of heights. It should have come as no surprise, of course, that our first challenge just had to be one that required me to dangle on a trapeze-like bar over the edge of that 150-foot-high bridge—facing the rocky, dry riverbed below and mountains and freeway maze beyond.

In the first challenge, the women competed against each other, and then the men took their turns. The first person up set the time standard the others would have to beat. The one with the slowest time would have to leave the show.

I breathed a small prayer as the crew hooked me into a safety harness and tethered me to a long cable that would allow me to fall almost all the way to the ground when I let go. I stepped out onto the metal platform placed as an overhang off the bridge. I reminded myself not to look down and wrapped my hands around that thin, slick metal rod. They had a camera attached to a bar on the helmet, giving an up-close and personal view of the fear on my face. My "last words" were, "God be with me. Oh, please."

And then the metal platform dropped out from underneath me. I thought of nothing except holding on. I blocked out the jeers and shouts of encouragement floating up from the crew and cast far below. Then slowly, my hands, slick with sweat, began to slip. I felt my fingers sliding off the bar until I felt myself plummeting toward the earth. On the way down, all I could hear was the rush of wind and my heart pounding in my ears. Then, just before I would have slammed into the ground, the cable, like a bungee cord, halted my fall, and I bounded up and down a few times before finding my feet planted on solid ground.

One after another, the contestants tried their best, but each one—the men and women—lost their grip faster than I did. I won the round by eight seconds. With memories of my brothers and boy cousins in mind, I was thrilled that I beat every one of the guys' times. But my satisfaction went far beyond that competitive accomplishment. I'd done it! I had faced my great fear of heights, and with God's help, I not only overcame that fear but had become the winner at the very thing I feared the most. I was ecstatic!

What would come next? I wondered, believing myself ready for any challenge. We were never told ahead of time what the next challenge would be. Our only preparation was a quick, cryptic message, like the one we got in our hotel rooms later the next day. "Ten o'clock tonight. You'll be eating something."

I dressed in jeans, a white shirt, and a red button-up sweater; clasped my gold cross necklace around my neck as my witness; and met the group inside the hotel lobby. Although we were friendly, we didn't say much to each other. We were all stressed-out. In game mode.

We piled into a van, where the crew blindfolded us, and the drive began. When we arrived, I still can't tell you today where we were. It was dark. There were broken concrete slabs all around, and bright can lights positioned to make the setting eerie. They asked us to walk on camera one at a time, spaced about ten feet apart, wearing a grim expression to create a weird dramatic vibe. They made us look all tough and serious.

The guys didn't seem to think very highly of me. I'm sure it was, at least in part, because of my petite size and quiet demeanor. One said, "I think there is a line Andrea won't cross. Andrea is too cute to get down and dirty for the fifty grand." He greatly underestimated my determination.

Although *Fear Factor* hadn't been around for very long, the episodes I'd seen included some pretty disgusting stuff. However, I must say that I think our food challenge pretty much took the prize as #1 in the gross category. We rolled a skee ball—like in a carnival game—and whichever target-like hole it landed in, that's how many of the item we'd be required to eat. Sadly, everyone got the number six.

Six what? I am not kidding when I say we had to eat *pig uterus*. Yes, ladies and gentlemen, we had to eat six pig uteruses in six minutes. Each pig uterus was at least a foot long and looked kind of like a curly strip of shiny, slimy pink rubber. The first guy, all cocky and sure of himself, tried to eat them too fast, stuffing them into his mouth until there was nowhere for them to go. We all thought he was going to hurl. He didn't. But he also didn't down those uteruses.

Then it was my turn. I tried. I really did. I got two down when the host said I had forty seconds left. I spit out what was left in my mouth and said, "I'm not shoving all that in in forty seconds."

"Sorry, Andrea," the host said.

"Dude. It's all good. I've got four less pig uteruses in my stomach. It's quite all right with me."

After I blew a kiss to Leslie—the remaining girl contestant—I walked off, certain at that point I was off the show. (If you refuse a challenge or cannot complete it, you forfeit your place on the show.) Once off camera, I was asked what I felt. I said, "No regrets. You only live once. Why not? This is going to be one of the best memories of my life." And I knew I meant it. I had proven to myself that I could finally put an end to the childhood labels of crybaby and fraidycat. I was not, in fact, a loser at all. I'd been given opportunities to do things I feared and had overcome those fears. The accomplishment of facing my fear of heights was, in particular, a welcomed gift.

Someone once asked what pig uterus tasted like. "Like rubber flesh that won't break down in your mouth like normal food does," I said. It was almost like it grew as I chewed—so disgusting. Not only did my intestinal world complain for days, but I couldn't eat pork for years.

Because none of the other contestants managed to eat the allotted pig uteruses, we were delighted to discover that the four of us could return the next day for the final challenge. The prize money had dropped to $25,000, an amount I could still happily accept.

The final challenge was another one that tested my fear of heights. A path of Plexiglas plates was suspended five floors above the lobby of a fancy downtown Los Angeles hotel—the Bon Adventure. We had to walk across them from one balcony to the other without holding on to anything. And we had to move quickly. It required balance as each plate had two steel cables threaded through them that helped stabilize them, yet keep them wobbly at the same time. My heart was in my throat, but having accomplished "Suicide Bridge," I knew I could do this. Though wobbly, I made it across and once again, I beat the guys! Leslie was the last to go, and her turn was after mine. Leslie beat me by seven seconds, and sadly, I lost the $25,000 prize.

I was disappointed. No question about it. I desperately could have used that money. Yet I was proud of myself. I came in such a close second. I wasn't the best. I didn't get first place. But I did beat out the boys! Something I could thank my brothers for—their taunts had made me tough. Besides, I won something more important—the realization that even a great fear could not hold me back if I set my heart on a goal.

I wasn't a victim; I wasn't even just a survivor. I was an overcomer who now had overcome labels that had stuck with me since childhood. I consciously released those old lies, and determined to step into being the fighter that was always in me. I could now see myself taking on a new perspective. Would I also be able to learn to truly *be* myself rather than bow to the pressure of being what others expected me to be? The answers to that question had not yet been tested.

Overall, it was a good experience, and I'm glad I did it, not to prove anything to others, but honestly to prove to myself that I could do something when I set my mind to it. It was all good. Well, except for the pig uterus. I could have done without that. But at least I always win the party game "Who has eaten the grossest food?" Even today I can beat the boys at that one.

Chapter 13

THE VOICE

Trust in the Lord with all your heart,
And lean not on your own understanding;
In all your ways acknowledge Him,
And He shall direct your paths.

PROVERBS 3:5–6 NKJV

2001 had proven itself to be an important year of growth and change. Of worship and Bible study and fellowship and prayer. Of deep friendship with Christine and my roommate, Nancy—friendships rich in the bond of faith we shared. Of following God into new opportunities, exercising the fighter in me to fight for God's purposes rather than my own and then accepting his outcomes. By the spring of 2002 when my *Fear Factor* episode aired, I was well on my way to embracing whoever God wanted me to be and whatever challenges he placed in my path. I was growing into seeing myself through the lens of God's love for me—at least to the degree I understood God's love at that point.

I did still steer clear, however, of any hint of a romance and concentrated on building up my clientele at Crunch Fitness rather than building up a social life. In fact, I had been working with my client Paddy Cullen for about a year when, in the spring of 2002, she made me an offer I couldn't refuse.

"I told you I'm producing the movie *Down with Love*, starring Ewan McGregor and Renée Zellweger, didn't I?" she said, somewhat short of breath because we were talking between lunges. I nodded with interest as I counted out her movements. Both stars' careers were blazing hot at the time, and anticipation of the movie was running high.

"Ewan is very lean right now and will need to buff up for his role. Would you want to do it?"

Wow, did I ever! Two of my favorite actors, and I was going to train one of them? I was ecstatic, and my enthusiasm grew when she told me what the pay would be, especially when I learned I'd also be hired to train Ewan's wife, as well as some of the other producers. This was about to become the most consistent income I had ever had in my life. Not only would I have enough money to meet all my expenses, but I'd finally have room to breathe.

My excitement for what Jesus was doing in my life at this point was spilling over into everything I did. Simply sharing what Jesus was doing in my life with others had become my first priority. I couldn't *not* share Jesus, and I was now praying specifically that God would use me to tell others about this amazing relationship with him.

I was excited when I was invited to Ewan's house for his and his wife's training sessions (and to meet his two adorable children). Ewan was wonderfully easy to be with—lighthearted, warm, and charming. During arm curls and squats, we spoke freely of our interests, and it seemed as natural as breathing to tell him how God was transforming my life. His gracious response of genuine interest built my confidence and bolstered my desire to share my faith with others. I was living in awe of how God answers prayers.

One Sunday after church, Christine and I grabbed coffee and were talking at a picnic table in the little park in Cross Creek near the church, when Pamela Anderson walked by with her two young sons. I hadn't seen her since she had been so kind to me at the mansion, but I did not mention that as I introduced her to Christine.

Christine struck up a conversation about her boys, mentioning that she taught kids in Sunday school at Malibu Vineyard right down the street, and that I often helped her.

Pamela showed a genuine interest and seemed grateful. The following week, she came to church with her boyfriend, Kid Rock. I hadn't seen him since appearing by his side in the music video in my pre-Christian days. A few weeks later, I was walking into church carrying my New Believer's Bible and spotted her in the parking lot. I suddenly felt an inner urging to walk over and give it to her. I was so nervous and scared and wasn't sure at first if the urge came from God, so I prayed, "Lord, what am I supposed to do?"

I didn't doubt the answer. I walked up to her, said hello, and said, "I feel like I'm supposed to give this to you."

"Oh my word! You're so sweet. Thank you." She seemed genuinely moved.

I've not seen Pamela since that day, but the memory points me to that very special experience of following through on God-given urges to reach out to people—a practice I try to continue to this day.

God wasn't through with surprises for me. It seems now, looking back, as if he was working me up to a greater sensitivity and willingness to hear and obey him.

One night I was at Media Fellowship International (MFI), a Bible study for Christians in the entertainment industry, when David White appeared out of nowhere. I hadn't seen him for about a year. We made eye contact, and I noticed two things. First, he was really good-looking— something I hadn't paid much attention to when he was pursuing me the year before. And second, he was looking at me very strangely. Shocked. A weird expression on his face.

It seems that just that afternoon he had flown in from Vegas, and while waiting for his bag at the airport, he turned to his friend and said, "I've got to go back to Malibu to see about that girl Andrea." The thought had simply come to him out of nowhere. So when he saw me just a few hours later, it seemed like more than just a coincidence.

"What are you doing here?" he asked.

I smiled at the way he asked the question, as if he needed some explanation for my presence. "Korey, the second assistant director on the movie *Down with Love*, invited me," I said.

"Oh? So what are you up to these days?" he said.

"I'm still working at Crunch Fitness, and right now I'm training Ewan McGregor for his role in the movie."

Today David laughs when he recalls telling his friend Jeff about our conversation. Jeff told him, "Man, you don't stand a chance against 'Ben' Kenobi of *Star Wars*! Ewan McGregor? You are *so* out of your league." Leave it to the boys! Obviously he had no idea that Ewan was a happily married man.

He asked a few polite questions about Ewan's role, and then, clearly wanting to extend the conversation, he asked, "What else have you been up to?"

The strangest, most surprising words came out of my mouth. "I don't know. I'm just ready to find my husband."

I probably looked as shocked as he did. *Why in the world did I say that?* I thought. Especially when I certainly was *not* looking for a husband. I was nowhere near ready for one. I wanted the floor to open up and swallow me whole.

You know how sometimes when you say something that doesn't come out right and when you try to fix it, everything you add just makes it worse? That's what happened. "Oh!" I said. "Uh . . . I, uh . . . That was so weird."

He stared at me, cleared his throat, and tried to talk, but he managed only to croak out some awkward response.

This was going from bad to worse. "Um," I said, "Christine and I and some of our friends take moonlight hikes up to Paseo Miramar. We plan to go tomorrow night. Want to come?" He immediately mentioned how much he loved hiking.

FEASTING ON FRIENDSHIP

The next evening, he showed up at our meeting point. He was wearing some old-school, nylon-snap breakaway basketball pants. Clearly, this guy was no hiker. But dorky breakaway basketball pants or not, I enjoyed having him on the hike. We didn't spend the entire time together, but enough that I could ask him some questions about his faith. He'd grown up Mennonite, which I knew nothing about, and had been a Christian his entire life. For the first time, I allowed him to see a little of the real me. And I watched as he interacted with others. It was good to see how kind and friendly he was. I didn't feel preyed on. Given my history, that was a very good thing. He was engaging; he was a talker; he was very charismatic; and impressively, he asked great questions and was a very good listener. And clearly he was interested in me.

At the end of the hike, when we got in our separate cars, he rolled down his window. "Wanna get a bite to eat?" He gave me a hopeful smile.

"Can't. Gotta get up at five and be at work by six."

He kept smiling—direct and unwavering—as if trying to think of something else to say and not coming up with anything. Finally he said, "Okay. See you later."

We went our separate ways, and as I was driving home to Brentwood, a voice said, *That's your husband.*

Weird. It wasn't as if I had said it to myself. It had come out of nowhere. I had no idea what to do with the thought. I drew no conclusions, and knowing that friendship was all I felt, I assured myself I would keep our relationship where it belonged—as new friends.

A few weeks later, David called. "Hey, some girls from Texas who are part of a Christian dance ministry are going to perform on the Third Street Promenade in Santa Monica by Venice Beach. Want to go?"

"Christian dancers? Okay . . . sure, why not? Yeah."

"My friend Jeff owns a restaurant around the corner from there. We can head over and grab a bite afterward."

That evening, after the performance, we chatted as we walked toward Jeff's restaurant. David is a gregarious, inquisitive person, someone who will ask anyone anything, wanting to get to know people on a deeper level. I liked that about him—until he asked, "Why did your parents get a divorce?"

Way too personal. That was a long and painful story I wasn't interested in sharing. He was wise enough to pick up on my response and shift the conversation to lighter, less personal topics.

Once we took our seats at Jeff's fine restaurant, it dawned on me that an invitation to check out a street ministry was progressing to a full five-course meal and a long conversation. What a sneaky guy! I was looking for a casual night with a friend, and he had planned a date. But the truth was, the food and conversation were great, and when dinner was over, we somehow found ourselves in a "tribute to the 70s" club next door. I felt no need to impress him, looking at it as just goofing around with a friend, so I let out my silliness and started dancing ridiculously crazy—with exaggerated disco moves, hair flying all over, goofy expressions. He seemed delighted and followed suit. Soon we were both laughing until our sides hurt. We laughed . . . and laughed . . . and laughed. And then my shoe broke! We could not stop laughing, even as the evening came to an end and I hobbled back to his car dragging one foot so I wouldn't lose my shoe. It was so fun to connect on that level, realizing we had the same sense of humor. Laughter, goofy dancing, and a shoe malfunction made the night magical.

As the evening ended, however, despite the fun, I still had no interest in taking our relationship up a notch. But I did realize I had never felt more comfortable with a guy. For the first time in my life, I wasn't trying to impress or fit in or be what he expected me to be. *And even if we did go out to dinner and a disco*, I told myself, *we weren't on a date. As far as I'm concerned, we are just friends.*

We hung out a lot after that. David (I later learned) assumed we *were* dating; I assumed we were not. I did enjoy his company—a lot. But as a young believer of only about eighteen months, with such a checkered history with men, I simply wasn't ready to find myself—my heart— distracted by a man. I had been there, done that, and I didn't want a repeat. Building an intimate relationship with God—keeping my relationship with him as the most important one in my life—had to be my top priority.

About a year before, David had played a leading role as identical twins (John and Jeremiah) in a film called *Mercy Streets*. There had been a lot of hype about the film, as critics liked it a lot, so expectations had run high when it was first released. This was the film that David hoped would catapult him to the next level—into all he dreamed of for his acting career. But it hadn't done particularly well in theatres. It was a faith-oriented film, but it had come out years before the current wave of interest in faith-based movies.

In the time since then, he'd received a few offers for roles, but he felt like his acting career was over—so much so, in fact, that he began to seek out alternatives. A friend tried to teach him how to edit movie trailers. But that was so far outside of David's gifting that it was about the worst thing in the world for him to do for a living. Still, it paid. Ever the optimist, he tried to convince himself it was adding a new skill set to his industry experience. During this period, our outings became less frequent, which, given his disappointment, I understood completely. After all—we were just friends.

One day, for a reason I couldn't explain, I felt powerfully impressed to call and encourage him.

"How are you?" I asked, not in a casual tone, but genuinely wanting to know the real answer. He seemed to appreciate my call, and we talked for a long while. As I listened, I realized how desperately he needed that call. When I hung up, I was so moved that God had let me know David needed me that night. I was still new to the leading of the Holy Spirit, especially when it came to discovering that God could use me to minister to others.

The spiritual connection with David continued to grow. A few times, when I was praying with my Bible open to a Scripture, David called, saying, "Hey, I was just reading this Scripture and wanted to share it with you." It happened to be the same Scripture! Coincidence?

The night before he was to leave for Texas to do some reshoots for a Chuck Norris film—*Bells of Innocence*, in which he was acting—David invited me to his place to make me dinner, so that, he explained by phone, we could have a serious conversation. This concerned me. I respected him so much and adored our friendship. But I also sensed he was at a point in his life where he was looking for a wife. On my way over, I prepared to suggest we stop hanging out so much because I didn't want to keep him from finding his wife. But as the evening began, it quickly became clear that, though I was ready to run, he was ready to commit. My plans were far different than God's plans!

"I'm interested in dating you, Andrea," he said. "There's something really special about you. Your love for the Lord is clear and strong. You seek out a much deeper spiritual level than most of the actors or pretty people I see in Hollywood. That's more than just interesting to me; it's important."

He learned forward to kiss me, but I pulled back. He sat back, a questioning look in his gentle eyes, waiting, knowing I was about to speak.

I put my hands in my lap where he couldn't reach them. "I love hanging out with you, David, but I know you're looking for a wife, and I don't think I'm that wife."

I braced myself, concerned my honesty might make him angry—as it had Mike and Scott and Joe. Instead, he responded quite differently. "Okay. I get that." He nodded, as if confirming something to himself.

I don't remember if we ended the evening early or if we watched a movie on TV. But whatever it was, I ended that evening assured that this was okay. No stress. No pressure. Simply acceptance.

He left for Texas as planned.

And then he didn't call me. Not that night or the next or the entire week.

It was then I realized—I missed him. A *lot*.

I invited Christine over to watch David's movie *Mercy Streets*, which I rented from Blockbuster. As I watched it, I realized how much I cared for him—more than I thought. "Christine, I *miss* him."

Christine started to cry. "Andrea," she said, reaching for a tissue, "I think he's your husband."

Then I started weeping. "I think you're right," I whispered as a sense of awe settled on me. We then had a moment of the Holy Spirit hitting us like a torrential downpour of tears and supernatural peace. It was one of those God moments that I can never quite explain other than to say that I knew God's presence, intense and powerful.

When David returned, he did call, and hearing his voice lit up my heart. God had so nurtured and healed me for that year between our very first meeting and our second. And now God had let me know: he was giving me a gift. It was time. Time to relish a new, pure love.

This time I didn't hesitate to accept an invitation for a date—a mutually acknowledged date. We agreed to go to the Derby to go dancing. And it was there that I—*yes, I*—initiated our first kiss.

Chapter 14

FROM FEAST
TO FAMINE

Not that I have already obtained all this, or have already
arrived at my goal, but I press on to take hold of that for
which Christ Jesus took hold of me.

PHILIPPIANS 3:12

Despite the joy of God's presence in my life in that first year and a half as
a new believer, not every experience was sweet. It became clear that the
connection between my health and my relationship with food, always
fragile, was going to be an ongoing battle. I was confused about the whole
food thing. (I still am as I navigate through uncomfortable health issues.)
I wasn't discouraged at first, though. After committing my life to Jesus,
I went back to many of the practices of the faith-based diet program,
because it had been helpful in reminding me of the importance of daily
prayer and surrender for appetite and food issues.

At the time, my eating issues weren't to the point of being debilitating, but they were obviously still with me as an ever-present preoccupation
with the relationship between food, fitness, and well-being. When to eat,
what to eat, how much to eat, calories consumed, calories burned, energy
level, strength, and stamina—all were forever vying for and consuming

far too much of my attention and effort. I was working a lot of hours, wasn't sleeping well, and was running on caffeine. Since my anorexia, I had grown accustomed to running on fumes, as if to do so was normal. During my *Survivor* and *Fear Factor* periods, I had pumped up my stamina with those extra snacks, because I'd been trying to gain weight, but afterward I quickly fell back, often feeling weak and sick. Not enough to stop working or stop my fitness training, but enough that it took effort to just push through it all.

Then I met Timothy, a Christian whose nutritional regimen was just the opposite of mine. I liked the fact that he was a believer who emphasized that God's ways are good and that he gives us good things to eat. So when he offered to help me restore my health by cleansing and rebooting my very broken system, I agreed. Timothy ate raw foods almost exclusively. He would eat animal protein, but only if it was raw or seared so the enzymes were still intact. All of his fruits and vegetables were eaten raw, with a few exceptions that could be steamed without diminishing their nutritional value.

He began by taking me to farmers markets to help me get a new vision for food and stock up on the good stuff. He got me to switch to eating about 75 percent raw foods, and for added protein, he had me eat sushi and seared beef. I knew I needed help, and for a while, I followed his advice, even to the point of consuming the supplements and herbs he gave me.

In an effort to regain my health, I listened to his advice not to eat anything out of a bottle or a can for a while. Sound extreme? It was. But don't get the impression I was highly disciplined or devotedly adhering to his strict diet. The truth is, the eating disorder that had plagued me for years was still as much a temptation as ever, and I often caved—like nearly inhaling a Butterfinger candy bar, for instance. Most of the time, I felt deprived—and as anyone with an eating disorder can tell you, deprived is not a good place to be.

SELF-IMPOSED FAMINE

As David and I grew in our friendship, before my turning point of deciding to date him, I had confided in him about my past battles with anorexia and my ongoing preoccupation with food, just as I had to Christine. I'd even told him about my lowest point while living with my dad in San Diego, too weak at seventy-eight pounds even to get out of bed. David and Christine both were supportive and encouraging, commending me for the balance I had found over the three years since that time, and cheering me on in my commitment to pray and seek God's strength. I found it troubling and discouraging, however, that having the Holy Spirit within me and praying for relief from the struggle weren't eradicating this challenge from my life.

Wasn't I supposed to be living a victorious life? *This* wasn't victory.

And then, to my horror, a new challenge surfaced.

It started that very week of my first kiss with David at the Derby. He was at my place—which I shared with Nancy—and he was hungry, so I fixed him a tuna sandwich with the real mayonnaise that Nancy kept on hand. I hadn't eaten real mayo in years. After David left, I was hungry and ate the leftover tuna with corn chips. At least I *began* by eating them, but when they were gone, I was overcome with the urge to binge on the mayo—which I did. Then my mind latched on to the idea of that fat and oil invading me. Immediately I ran to the bathroom and forced myself to vomit—something I had never done before in my life.

I had no idea that a battle unlike any I'd ever faced had begun.

No one wants to have an eating disorder. Like any addiction, it sneaks in, telling you little lies that are believable. For many years, anorexia had given me the illusion that I had control over my life. It seemed that if only I was strong enough to control what I ate and how much exercise I did, then I'd have the power to control other things in my life too.

Bulimia presented a different lie for me. It promised a sensation of relief, though it was never clear to me from what. Anxiety? Discomfort from facing change? Fear of intimacy—not of my physical body but of my soul? Internal conflict that I could not identify? I honestly didn't comprehend what I felt compelled to find relief from—only that the urge for relief felt overpowering and inevitable.

Purging became a new habit—compelling, consuming, seemingly irresistible. When I purged my stomach of its contents, I felt a sense of emotional cleansing and release. It calmed my feelings of confusion, anxiety, and being overwhelmed by life. For a moment upon purging, a dopamine rush took place, a sense of "ah, now I'm better." Just as anorexia offered me the illusion of control and power, bulimia offered me the illusion of peace—a flood of sweet release from whatever churning discomfort was eating away at my heart.

I didn't dive happily into this new addiction. It was a slow, gradual descent as the lie of release took hold. About one week after my first purging, I felt the urge again. From then on, I purged about once a week, then once a day, and then, over a period of months, after nearly every meal. Then it became relentless, like something trying to kill me, and there were days it got so bad that I lost count of how many times I purged. The stress and tension would build inside me until I had to do something to make it go away. Alcoholics and drug addicts put something into their bodies to take away that tension and anxiety, but I, as a bulimic, was taking something out of my body to achieve the same sense of relief. But the things I was getting out were nutrition and sustenance.

I hated it. Oh, how I hated it. But I felt powerless to stop. The urge was so strong. The entire ordeal confused me. I was an on-fire, Bible-believing, tongues-speaking, crazy-for-Jesus girl. How could this awful thing be alive and well—and growing—inside me? How could I be powerless over this horrific desire while still loving my Jesus with every fiber of my being?

When the bulimia began, I was about a year and a half into my faith, but I wasn't plugged into a solid relationship with a spiritually mature mentor or Christian leader. My lifetime of living in emotional isolation from others in my self-protective, imagined self-sufficiency hadn't melted away or even yet been exposed to me in the brief period of my newfound faith. I was still new to discovering the character of God, the power of his Word, and the strength and support I could derive from Christian friendships. But now, I was willingly repeating an awful, destructive habit that made me deeply ashamed.

So I kept it secret.

But shame thrives in secrecy. Tucked away in a dark internal place, hidden from the light of openness and communication, it expands, deepens, and, worst of all, lies. Skillfully.

Shame became my shadow, following me everywhere, whispering to me daily, *You are a failure, unworthy of God's love, too weak and powerless to be a good Christian.*

Saddest and most distressing of all was that I faced this battle alone during the very time of the thrill and joy of falling in love with David. How could two such opposite forces be at work in me at the same time? I didn't have a clue.

I had revealed to David what my life was like before I became a Christian—my family's unhealthy patterns, my teen years of drugs and dating and experimenting with my fair share of guys, my struggles with control that led to the devastating years of anorexia, and finally the Playboy Mansion and the partying years that brought me to the end of my rope.

Was there a bit of culture shock for him? Certainly. David's life experiences had been drastically different from mine. His Mennonite childhood had been very sheltered by comparison. He laughed as he told me he had seen only one movie growing up. He went to see *Grease* when he was eight years old. His friend's parents had taken him with their kids, and he purposefully didn't tell his parents. While watching, he kept worrying throughout the film, *Oh no, will this send me to hell?*

He recounted his journey from growing up in Kansas to being a student at Moody Bible Institute. At nineteen and still an earnest, Jesus-loving kid, he had arrived in Hollywood with a passion to act and then landed a role in a TV show within his first six months.

The most beautiful discovery for me in our long conversations was to see a man who not only loved God with his whole heart, but also felt a driving passion to use the power of movies to both introduce people to Jesus and help them grow closer to him. To find that this man held no judgment of or condemnation for me was such an unexpected gift. David knew far deeper than I did the depths of God's forgiveness, grace, and unconditional love. More than any other person I had ever met, he modeled those values in how he loved me.

How could I be experiencing such wonder with him and at the same time be hiding my pain? My shame ran deep. How could I be thriving in God's Word and a new life in Jesus and at the same time be purging my body of all the nutritious foods I'd been consuming, putting myself through a self-imposed famine? Wasn't I a new creation? Then why this torment? Didn't God delight in giving good things to his children? Then why wasn't he answering my prayers for deliverance? Didn't God's Word have authority? Then why didn't the Bible verses I was reading solve this problem?

I felt afraid—afraid that this wonderful new life of faith and this wonderful new romance would become yet two more losses in a life littered with them. Yet at the same time, God's presence had become so real and vibrant to me that I didn't doubt God's salvation of me. Such confusion and torment.

MOVIE MAKING

Weeks became a month, then two, then three. Then, one Sunday afternoon after church, as David and I had lunch together, he brought up an idea. I found it so exciting that it took my mind off the contemplation of the heaviness of the food in my stomach and the nagging thoughts of how long I'd have to wait until I could purge again.

"You know that movie, *Six, the Mark Unleashed*, that Kevin and I have been planning to start filming this December?" he said. (David and his dear friend, Kevin Downes, had been working together making Christian films for DVD release since 1996.)

"Of course," I said. "The one Stephen Baldwin is going to be in."

He nodded. "We're wondering if you'd be interested in working on it with us. Our budget is really small, so the pay will be modest, but we need someone to wardrobe the film, and we also have a small part you might want to consider." I could feel both excitement and fear bubbling inside me. I'd never wardrobed a film before, but the opportunity to focus on something new excited me. A client I had trained at Crunch was a costume designer, so I knew I could turn to her for advice. Working on a film can be an incredible experience in which great bonds often form between cast and crew, and I couldn't resist the opportunity to work with my best friend just as our new love was growing. It seemed too good to be true. So I dove in.

By the time we ended our four-week shoot in Visalia, California, we were falling in love. We loved acting and making movies together, and we loved the Lord. I was so grateful to God for this chance to work on a Christian film with a message that had eternal impact. What a contrast to my past! And David was not only pursuing his passion for ministry through entertainment, but he also had a woman by his side who adored and respected him.

And yet . . . I carried my dark secret with me. What a picture of the double life of addiction! There I was, binging and purging in tears and agony behind closed doors and then going out to shoot scenes, oversee wardrobe, and enjoy the love and laughter of God's work on the movie.

Finally, six long months after our first kiss, in complete desperation,

I made the decision to tell David. I had come to love him so deeply that I wanted total transparency, and I knew that secrets and transparency couldn't coexist. True love could only grow in honesty and openness. I would rather risk losing David altogether by telling him the truth than live in the shadows of the skeletons in my closet. Would I ruin our relationship by exposing that I had been keeping an awful secret?

Chapter 15

TO THE EDGE OF TRUST

I do not understand what I do. For what I want to do I do
not do, but what I hate I do.

ROMANS 7:15

I glanced quickly at the mirror while waiting for David's knock on the front door of the apartment I still shared with Nancy. Tonight, knowing for certain I'd soon be crying, I'd gone easy on my eye makeup. My medium-length blonde hair hung in loose curls for our casual date. The mirror told me I looked totally put together. But mirrors see only the outside. I took a few slow, deep breaths to steady my racing heartbeat as I studied my reflection, willing myself to follow through on my decision to expose the hidden darkness.

Moments later, as David held open the door of his white Ford Explorer for me, I couldn't help but meet his adoring eyes. I smiled back despite the huge knot in my stomach. He had no idea. Not a clue. *I must be a better actor than I know*, I thought sarcastically as I slid into the front seat. *He's anticipating a romantic date, while I'm probably about to ruin our whole relationship.*

"Why don't we get a bite to eat at Gaucho Grill before the movie?" David said as we pulled out of the lot. "I'm starved."

"Sure. Sounds perfect," I said, my stomach lurching at the thought of food. My heart began racing again, and I noticed I had a death grip on the car door handle. I forced myself to slowly ease my grip and relax my hand. *There's no way I'll make it through dinner,* I reasoned. *I've got to tell him before we eat.*

While my thoughts battled within, I, the queen of pretense, chatted with David about the reviews we'd read of the movie we were about to see, and we compared opinions on other roles we'd seen the cast play. We loved to talk movies—our shared passion.

By the time we pulled into the restaurant parking lot, my palms were clammy. As soon as he turned off the ignition, David turned to me, that eager boyish grin clearly anticipating a relaxed, enjoyable evening, and his gaze was so innocent and unsuspecting.

"You look beautiful tonight," he said.

It was hard to believe a full six months had passed since our first kiss—six months of feeling deeply seen, cherished, loved. But not completely open—not on my part, for it also marked six months of my secret bulimia. I ached to be honest with him, to take that huge step, knowing the only way forward was to reveal my secret. The thought of the ugliness I was about to describe made my stomach lurch again and triggered my tears. I tried to blink them away, but too late. The image of the smiling actor dissolved.

"Andrea, what's wrong?"

"David, these six months have flown by. I love being with you."

He started to speak and then stopped, knowing intuitively not to push me.

"I need to tell you something," I began.

"You can tell me anything." he said. I'm not sure what I expected his expression to be—alarm maybe, worry for sure. But I wasn't prepared for this look—one of optimism. Confidence mixed with empathy. *Lord, is this man as good and true as he seems? I guess I'm about to find out.*

"I know you remember, when we were just getting to know each other, before we even started dating, that I told you about my past with anorexia."

He nodded and said, "And when we started to date, I told you that whatever you faced, we would face together. Remember?"

I studied his face, wishing I could internalize his confidence. "Now there's something else . . ." My voice was trembling. I hated feeling so weak. "I've been—" I couldn't bring myself to say it.

He waited in silence, his hand stroking mine.

"I've been throwing up." I swallowed hard and pulled my hand away. "I'm struggling with bulimia." I struggled to control my tears so that I could finish, my words spilling out quickly now. "It started the very first night we kissed. I had never done it before then. Never. And I don't understand why I started then. It's beyond my control. I keep promising myself I'll never do it again, but then I do. And it has gotten worse. I keep asking God to stop it. Pleading with him to deliver me from it. But my prayers aren't working. Why? What's wrong with me?"

David sat looking at me as he stroking my hair. "I'm here for you," he said. "It's gonna be okay, hon. You know I love you—completely. No matter what. And God loves you, no matter what. We'll get through this."

"I'm so confused," I said. "I thought when someone was saved, they had power over their temptations. I mean, after all, I'm a Bible-believing, faith-filled Christian. I have the Holy Spirit in me, right? I've confessed this over and over, but it has some kind of grip on me that just won't break. I feel disgusting. Useless. Worthless. I keep failing."

"Andrea, listen." He pulled me closer and looked directly into my eyes, his face filled with gentleness and his voice reassuring. "I love you. I'm with you in this. All the way. We *will* get through this."

A huge sense of relief settled over me—not necessarily because I shared his confidence that we would get through it, but because I had told him. The secret was out. And if David wasn't going to abandon me, then surely God wouldn't either, because God loved me even more than

David did. All my life I'd faced my heartaches and hardships on my own. Now here I was, a believer for only two years, and God had given me a man who was promising to walk with me through this.

Something stirred in me that I barely recognized at first—*hope*.

Yet I knew there was a fight ahead of me, a battle I believed was falling on my shoulders alone.

David sounded so optimistic I'd get past this. But he had never watched my body waste away to a walking skeleton. If my confessions and prayers hadn't worked so far, what was going to make the difference? What would break my urge—my compulsion—to keep repeating the very thing I didn't want to do?

I didn't know the answer, but there in the car with David, I knew something I hadn't known just moments ago. I had stepped out of my "all put together" mask in front of David and discovered that I was loved without condition, just as I was.

With David, I could be myself and still be loved—unconditionally loved. Without needing to be a winner. Without being smart or strong, without taking on crazy risks like riding on some ATV, without acting sexy and feigning attraction like in a bikini bar, without looking perfect and delivering every phrase flawlessly like at some audition. I could simply be myself, and David still loved me. And I knew then that this love was enough to enable me to take one more step—whatever that step might be.

I was such a young Christian back then that I didn't know God had me by the hand and was about to walk me through my first few lessons of Faith 101.

God often doesn't show us what lies ahead. Our choice when faced with the seemingly impossible is to decide which direction we walk—toward God or away from him. In choosing truth-telling over secret-keeping, I'd taken a huge step in the right direction. David's faith response, his love for me, and his confidence that together we would get through this encouraged me to move forward in the faith that God *would* act, even when I could not imagine how or when.

I had no idea at the time (and thank the Lord I didn't!) that this was a lesson I'd still be learning—trying to learn—this many years later while writing this book. That day, I believed the time would come when I'd trust God fully, 100 percent, no matter what. I know better now. Today, I believe that as long as we're living on this side of heaven, God is *always* at work, taking us by the hand and leading us all the way *to the end of our trust*, to that point where the next step we take is once again just beyond our sight. For this is how faith grows.

GROWING IN GOD'S DELIVERANCE

A few days later, I sat with Christine at her mom's restaurant in Newbury Park. I had just finished breaking the power of my secret shame by confessing my bulimia to her. Our mugs of coffee now sat cold on the table, next to two piles of tear-dampened tissues. "Christine," I said, new tears trickling down my checks, "I can't stop this alone. I need prayer."

Christine looked at me in her no-nonsense way and said, "Yes, we've got to get you prayed for."

The first name that popped into our heads was Janet, the tall, wise, spitfire associate pastor at Malibu Vineyard. Janet led mission trips and ministered to others through biblical counseling and was a mighty prayer warrior. Her beautiful face sprinkled with freckles and her head of curly, flaming red hair attested to the fiery strength that lay beneath. On a Monday afternoon, I stepped into her office with Christine, feeling ashamed and uncertain, but eager for help.

Janet sat down on a sofa, and we took our seats on a couple of over-stuffed chairs flanked by tables on either side, each holding a box of tissues. She was direct, yet gentle—a powerful combination for a woman in ministry. "Tell me what's going on," she said immediately. No small talk. She just went straight to the Lord's work.

I described what had been happening over the past six months. How the ferocity of the bulimia held me so firmly that I couldn't get away. I told her the urge was so powerful that it was present even at that moment. If I could eat and purge that very moment, I would.

She leaned forward, looking me directly in the eye. "Andrea, the power of God is far greater than he who is attacking you. Do you believe this?"

I nodded.

"We're going to pray. Do you realize that what you're engaged in is spiritual warfare?"

"Absolutely."

"Let me do the praying. Your job is just to receive the healing God gives you."

Then she prayed in the Spirit and took authority over my bulimia and my addiction. As she prayed, her voice rose in righteous vigor. Words were tumbling from her lips, verses of Scripture pouring out of her so fast that I couldn't believe anyone could have so much of it memorized. She spoke words of God's might and power, his purity and cleansing, his unending forgiveness, his dominion over death and evil and temptation. "By the authority of God's Holy Word and the blood of Jesus, I come to you, Father, on behalf of Andrea. We stand against the lies and tricks of the enemy. We claim your power and your truth, demanding this evil to flee in front of your Holy Name."

Scripture after Scripture continued through her prayers. The words of God himself, revealed through Scripture, rained down on me, flooded me, swept through me. I could hear God's power, feel it, and know it for what it was: my weapon. The weapon Janet was using against this ugliness that had seized my body for its use. I don't know how long we were there. But time no longer mattered, because we were in the presence of a holy God who loved me deeply and desperately.

"I command the spirit of unworthiness, the spirit of bulimia, the spirits that are not of the Lord to come out of this girl and be gone!"

I suddenly felt drained yet refilled as a peace and joy that I hadn't felt for months surged through me. The urge to shame myself by purging had vanished. That ever-present, overpowering, ugly urge was gone. Gone. Gone! I hadn't realized how much heaviness and oppression I'd been under until it vanished.

I raised my face to heaven, raised my hands in worship, and poured out my thanks to him who delivered me. When I walked out of the church and into the brilliant California sunshine that afternoon, I knew I no longer carried bulimia with me. It had been snatched from its hiding place and banished from my sight.

That day in February 2003, I had been given a glimpse of the perfect power of our perfect God. Even the memory is so powerful that a silent stillness falls over my soul as I remember it well over a decade later.

Now here is what is so intriguing. More than intriguing—mystifying, puzzling, even agonizing and infuriating! But as I write this, I celebrate this truth even while I confess it was painful to discover. In the next chapter, you will see that the deliverance from bulimia I received that day gave me one year of freedom. You will see that the bulimia did return. And that when it did, God chose *not* to use immediate supernatural intervention. He chose quite a different path, in a vastly different time frame.

As God's Word says in 1 Corinthians 13:12, "For now we see only a reflection as in a mirror; then we shall see face to face. Now I know in part; then I shall know fully, even as I am fully known." Since those days, I've come to understand far more about God's *now* and *then*. He is always the same God, above time, but while we live on this earth, we are subject to time. The perfect time—when we are face to face with God—*has not yet come.* We live in a world where our mirrors show only shadowy reflections. There is so much we do not yet "know fully."

Was I a child in my faith back in 2003 compared to where I am today? Yes, I was. But I believe I am still a child in my faith compared to the mature woman of faith I will be when Jesus welcomes me to his throne. That perspective eluded me at the time of my deliverance in Janet's office that Monday. On that day, a powerful prayer warrior prayed over me, and I was delivered, leading me to conclude that God miraculously, dramatically, supernaturally intervenes and delivers us from overwhelming temptation *when the right prayer warrior prays the right words*. Over time, God would teach me that his work is not limited to our formulas or our time frames.

Many long walks remained ahead of me that would take me to the edge of my trust—with my hand in the hand of Jesus. And I am sure many are yet to come. This is a foundational understanding I am exploring to this day. I believe it is a mysterious truth we must embrace to effectively do battle with perfectionism in our very unfinished lives.

Chapter 16

THE ROLE OF
A LIFETIME

But you are a chosen people, a royal priesthood, a holy
nation, God's special possession, that you may declare
the praises of him who called you out of darkness into
his wonderful light. Once you were not a people, but now
you are the people of God; once you had not received
mercy, but now you have received mercy.

1 PETER 2:9–10

As an actor, I must confess that of all the roles I've played in my lifetime,
the role of wife is undoubtedly the greatest challenge I've ever taken on.
(A less honest book might have said *joy* rather than *challenge*!) But be that
as it may, I am a very grateful woman, because within a few months of my
dramatic deliverance from bulimia, our understanding of love leaped to
whole new levels, and David proposed. My faith was growing; my hopes
for our future together were soaring; and a deeper love for God and for
David truly took hold in my heart.

To this day, I am beyond amazed and grateful that God chose David
to be my partner in the discovery of the power of love. We were soon to
discover that love—like faith—is strengthened when it is stretched to
its very edges, and it grows the most when we choose to step just beyond

what seems to be our own love limits—something David and I have come to know from lots of personal experience.

When, on July 20, 2003, we stepped into our roles as wife and husband, I had complete confidence in God as the perfect Casting Director. But in all transparency, almost immediately I began to suspect that God had either accidently handed us the wrong script or had cast the wrong people.

Now, years later, I can testify that God knew exactly what he was doing. The problem wasn't God's script or casting; it was just that the actors he had chosen were going to need some highly intensive direction. Let's just say we weren't exactly naturals at this marriage thing.

The same is true, I am still discovering, for us as believers. God knows who he is calling, the roles we are created to play, the challenges we will be called to face, and the contributions we will make in his eternal kingdom. But we must grow into our roles—big-time! In my case, I see now that God was absolutely brilliant to cast David as my husband and Ethan, Ocean, and Everson as our children, for within the White family that God has been building, God has taught me more about growing up in my faith and growing into my place in his kingdom than I've learned through any other source. Small wonder that God uses the imagery of family throughout Scripture.

A GARDEN WEDDING

Our wedding day was magical—everything I had ever hoped it would be and more. We held the ceremony in the lovely brick courtyard garden of a restaurant. Rose petals covered the center aisle, which was flanked by white chairs filled with loved ones and friends. One of the most precious moments of the day, for me, was when David and his brother played their violins during the ceremony. My dad gave me away—as tender a moment as I had dreamed. My mom, as beautiful as ever, simply glowed in joy for me from her honored position in the front row alongside my stepdad at the time, and Grandma and Grandpa Bahr looked on lovingly from just behind her. My brothers Jason and Josh, to whom by now I'd grown close, were impeccably handsome as ushers, and having them play a part in my special day meant the world to me. And seeing aunts and uncles and cousins who had traveled to join the celebration assured me that my childhood perceptions of teasing and bullying were long buried in my distant past.

Mom had flown out a few months prior to look at wedding venues with us. I'd been rushing around doing wedding preparations, so David had volunteered to pick Mom up at the airport. He still says he could have recognized her in an instant, even without their agreed-on spot to meet curbside outside of baggage claim.

"She looks so much like you," he told me later that day. "She's lovely. And she has the same kind of gentle sweetness about her that you do." He went on tell me how she surprised him by being so open during the ride. "She began telling me how happy she was for you," he said, "and then she started to cry. She said she felt terrible about not being a better mother to you and that she is filled with regrets. But most of all, she is so happy for us now and wants the very best for us. I hadn't been sure what to expect, but this was awesome. I couldn't have hoped for a better first meeting."

And sure enough, Mom's genuine love for me shined on my wedding day. It meant a lot simply to enjoy the present moments with her.

We stepped out of the 108-degree July heat into the cool of the restaurant for the reception, where, during the first dance of bride and groom, David glided me across the dance floor so that I felt I was floating. Then Dad extended his arm for me to join him in the traditional father-daughter dance. Everything about that day was far lovelier than I had even dared to dream.

BEING BUILT INTO A SPIRITUAL HOUSE

The apostle Peter could have been describing my spiritual journey when he wrote in 1 Peter 2:2–3, "Like newborn babies, crave pure spiritual milk, so that by it you may grow up in your salvation, now that you have tasted that the Lord is good." Yes! That's a perfect description of my baby steps right through my courtship with David and my deliverance from bulimia. From my stoplight encounter with God at the intersection in 2000 through our wedding day, I'd had experienced only three years as a Christian. That's a fairly short time for so many major life changes as I was growing up in my salvation.

But the verses that come after that—how can I say this with all due respect to Peter?—let's just say that what they describe sounds a whole lot easier than it really is: "As you come to him, the living Stone—rejected by humans but chosen by God and precious to him—you also, like living stones, are being built into a spiritual house to be a holy priesthood" (1 Peter 2:4–5).

I'm just going to say it: *Being built is hard.* Life is hard. Marriage is hard. Especially when, as living stones, David and I were both so hardheaded! But I wasn't expecting hard. I thought I'd been doing *hard* all my life, and that this was my time for *easy.* After all, my childhood and home life had been hard, and when I'd broken away from those and chosen my own way, I'd brought all kinds of *hard* on myself. I thought that the time had come for the happily-ever-after part, and those words about "being built into a spiritual house" sounded wonderfully, well, spiritual.

So, excitedly anticipating such bliss, I moved into David's little two-bedroom duplex in the Hollywood Hills that he owned with his good friend Brad. He lived above us, which might have been fine. In short, he and David had lived more like roommates than neighbors, and roommates and newlyweds don't necessarily blend well. Thankfully (for Brad as well, I'm sure), that situation lasted only about four months. We loved Brad (and still do), but as a brand-new couple, we wanted our home to be different from college dorm living.

In November 2003, David sold his part of the duplex, and we put a down payment on our first house in the Los Angeles suburb of Eagle Rock, between Glendale and Pasadena. It was a beautiful place—a brand-new, three-level house built into a hill. I was thrilled to call it home. Now I was ready for marital bliss!

And then, the unexpected. It was as if my body, feeling safe for the first time in my life, decided that now was a good time to crash. Utter exhaustion overcame me. The six months of bulimia had drained my stamina too much for me to continue personal training, and even though another six months had passed between my deliverance and our wedding, my adrenal glands were shot.

Without the personal training income, I took a part-time job at a makeup counter at a nearby mall, making $11.50 an hour at the Chanel makeup counter to help pay the bills and the mortgage. I quickly discovered I didn't like the job, intensified by the fact that my boss was a cocaine addict. Too many memories of the life I had left behind. Feeling ill and weak all the time didn't help. Even though my weakness was nowhere near as severe as it had been during my year in San Diego with anorexia, it was still severe enough that I had no energy to do anything. Before long, I quit my job.

Quitting my personal training at Crunch Fitness hadn't gone over well with David. Now quitting my part-time job was as welcome news as a bombshell. We had, after all, purchased a home with the assumption that I'd be working.

"You agreed to work," he said.

"I can't, David. I'm too sick."

Though David believed me, he was torn between his sympathy for me, his anger that I wasn't working, his fear that we wouldn't be able to pay the bills, and his worry over his new wife feeling sick nearly all the time. This wasn't what he'd had in mind for marriage. We began to bicker. Guilt, shame, unworthiness, and fear all came washing over me again—and as if that weren't bad enough, I began to have severe panic attacks. I didn't want this man I loved to be angry with me. Even though

I had little to no energy, once I combined his dashed expectations with my sense of guilt, anxiety, and defensiveness, I did find enough energy for one thing: fighting back. We were spiraling downward together.

This period of my life demonstrated to me some faulty thinking: We think that once we're living for God and not ourselves, when we're putting him first, that life will be easier and God will reward us. Yet it seemed to be just the opposite. Though the goodness in my life had grown, the battles had intensified since I had begun to call Jesus my Savior.

David was my best friend. But at that time in our lives, he was not what I wanted him to be as a life mate. Maybe even more frightening, I was not what he wanted me to be either. One doesn't overcome years of loss, along with the subsequent grasp for control, in just three years of baby steps of faith. Adjusting to married life is hard enough, but add in my past, my health issues, our precarious financial state, and the need for both of us to work at full throttle, and you have a recipe for marital trouble.

On the bright side (and yes, there was one), we still knew we loved each other. We still laughed at times and played and prayed together, and we still shared our passion for building a Christian movie ministry. So somewhere in the midst of all of that, we made our second film together, *The Moment After 2: The Awakening*.

A DOUBLE PUNCH

In January, I learned that the spiritual weight-loss program I had used when I lived alone a few years before was having a weekend event in Tennessee. I decided to attend. I had been delivered from bulimia for a year by then, with no recurrence, and I wanted help for my ongoing issues with food, fatigue, nutrition, and fitness—ever-present struggles. I arrived at the event filled with expectations and was touched by the many sweet people attending from all over the country. But I soon felt a disturbing uneasiness with the messages. The presenters were teaching that if we didn't completely overcome sin in our lives, sacrifices for our sins were no longer available and we would lose our salvation, and that living without sinning was fully possible for us to achieve. I felt confused and condemned for not being perfect. The Bible, I knew, teaches that Jesus died once for all our sins. Every one of our sins is covered by his blood—past, present, and future. I also understood that our sin nature is still at war within us and that God's grace covers that sin as he is at work to transform us until the day we meet him. As I sat listening to the messages, guilt, heaviness, and confusion descended on me. I returned home feeling even more lost and alone, imperfect and harshly judged by the harshest judge of all—myself.

David and I approached February 2004 with a mixture of anticipation and apprehension. My mom and grandparents were coming for a visit after the holidays. David had grown up in such a wonderful family, and he and I truly wanted our Christian marriage to have positive relationships with each of my parents. My relationships with my dad and brothers had continued to flourish, and my mom and I felt we had resolved as much as we could, considering the past.

This visit went well—no drama. But as much as I loved and wanted to see them, I found that their visit stirred many unresolved issues. I especially wrestled anew with my old sense of deep sadness over loss and abandonment, no doubt intensified by my fears over the tensions between David and me and my fears over God's judgment of me. Because of the ugly emotions already eating away at me, the line between present and past blurred. Memories swirled around my mother like a tornado, sucking me into the vortex again and again. I wasn't the hostess or "cookie-cutter Christian." I was so grateful for the visit, yet it surfaced so much sadness from my past. And I missed them so much when they left. *Will this pain never end?* I wondered. *I thought God's forgiveness had healed it all, but here it is again.*

The conference followed quickly by the visit with my mom delivered an intense double punch to my spirit that was already limping from my anxieties and the tensions with David. That old desire for release reared its ugly head, and I fell back into bulimia—I fell hard. I told David immediately, and he was supportive once again, with his "we can beat this" optimism, but as my bulimia dragged on from weeks to months, his sense of helplessness turned to frustration and then anger, which only deepened my destructive cycle. I cried out to God day and night, and to David as well, for help and deliverance, but finding no help and no answers, a deep spiritual isolation—from David and God—took hold.

When I opened my Bible, all I could see was God's wrath on me and that I would be punished. I could not find God's unconditional love, freedom, or peace. I just wept, believing I had failed not only once but now again—and this time, *after* God had delivered me. I feared I was too deep in the pit to ever make my way out.

I began seeing a Christian therapist, and it helped. For brief periods, I was able to stop the binging and purging. But oddly, during those times, I would become very angry. David couldn't understand why I was so kind and sweet to him when I was in the depths of bulimia, but an angry, temperamental woman when I wasn't. When I brought this up to the therapist, she said, "You're binging up and purging your pain and anger into the toilet—but your voice is going into the toilet too. You need to find your voice outside of bulimia. You need to learn to express your anger and pain openly."

But how could I, a perfectionist, willingly express the very anger and pain I saw as imperfect? Over the years, I had stuffed them so deep inside that, although submerged, they were all still there and had nowhere to go. As an avoider, I couldn't face the things that had happened to me, the choices made by others that had profoundly affected me, or the consequences of my own choices. It was too hard, too devastating, to face all these things, so I kept trying to rid myself of this burden by purging.

GETTING WORSE

Over the next year, I got steadily worse rather than better.

One evening, while David and I were arguing, he said, "I'm paying the grocery bill of a four-hundred-pound man!" His words humiliated me, and I became furious. I grabbed my boots from the floor next to my chair and threw them, along with a few choice words, and stormed out of the room, filled with shame and shocked by the truth in his words.

But as much as those words had hurt, he had a point. We had a twofold problem. I needed to stop binging and purging, and we needed me to earn some income. I took a job as a barista at a nearby coffee shop. It was a busy place, with a line frequently out the door, and though the pay was barely a drop in a bucket, my husband appreciated every drop I could contribute. But my bulimia went everywhere I did. I remember doing shots of espresso for energy after opening the café at 5:00 a.m., but being tired and wired on caffeine was a dangerous combination that induced crazy anxiety. Bulimia had already left me drastically dehydrated, and caffeine dehydrates too. I compensated for the dehydration with Gatorade and Emergen-C vitamin packets to replace my electrolytes so that I wouldn't die of a heart attack.

The boss was a controlling, driven man who once yanked my arm and yelled at me for not putting the straw on top of someone's iced tea. I wanted to fight back and spew my anger toward him—and I found that place where? In the toilet.

As unbelievable as it sounds, by now I was purging up to twenty-five times a day, hating myself more with every purge. When I wasn't purging, I would open God's Word, fall to my knees, and weep because I felt condemned. Certainly I was a sinner going to hell. After all, if I was saved, then why was I helpless to stop sinning? Why couldn't I stop this destructive pattern of self-abuse? I hated the fact that I was eager for

David to leave for work so I could binge and purge as much as I wanted in privacy. Not that I wouldn't still feel the shame in private; it would just be lessened by his absence.

I expected to die from the health complications of my eating disorder, because I could not break the cycle. And I very easily *could* have died—anorexia and bulimia have frightening health implications.

I was living the reality of Paul's words.

> I do not understand what I do. For what I want to do I do not do, but what I hate I do . . .
>
> So I find this law at work: Although I want to do good, evil is right there with me. For in my inner being I delight in God's law; but I see another law at work in me, waging war against the law of my mind and making me a prisoner of the law of sin at work within me. What a wretched man I am! Who will rescue me from this body that is subject to death?
>
> ROMANS 7:15, 21–24

And who *would* rescue me? I clearly couldn't rescue myself. My counselor couldn't. I tried Overeaters Anonymous but found no rescue there, and I finally realized that David could not rescue me either.

Paul provides the answer: "Thanks be to God, who delivers me through Jesus Christ our Lord!" (Romans 7:25).

I wasn't delivered yet from bulimia. Not even close. But I knew that God and only God could save me, and so I continued to plead with God for rescue.

AN UNEXPECTED GIFT

September 2005 arrived, marking my eighteenth month straight with bulimia. It was a typical month of dreading the days, as I felt continually bound by destruction and torment. I prayed, but received no answer, no peace, no freedom—and most nights, I cried myself to sleep.

Then, I realized that I was a few days late in my cycle. I wondered at first if it was because my body had been through hell and back because of the abuse of bulimia. I didn't suspect I was pregnant, because one of the unfortunate consequences of my long-ago relationships was precancerous cells on my cervix. In my early twenties, I had needed several surgeries, including the removal of part of my cervix, to eliminate those cells and had been told by my doctor that my chances of conceiving were greatly diminished. So why was I late?

Another week went by until one day, I bought a pregnancy test and raced home.

The world seemed to stop spinning when I stared at that little + sign on the stick. A breathtaking sense of awe settled over me. I placed my hand on my abdomen. There was a brand-new life in there. A tiny, vulnerable, precious little life. Part me and part David. A 100 percent unexpected, undeserved gift from God. Instantaneously, I felt an indescribable love for this tiny being.

My stomach lurched. I ran to the bathroom and threw up my lunch, and then the urge was gone. Completely gone. I knew it as certainly as I had known it in Janet's office when I was supernaturally delivered. God had heard my prayer and intervened with his power.

God had a role for me in his kingdom, and that role was not going to be taken away because of my weakness. His compassion for me was not diminished by my own inclination toward sin. God didn't hate me; he *loved* me. Not only did he have a plan to pull me out of the pit of hell in the midst of sin and brokenness; he also *blessed* me. Such a good, good Father. I could have died, as anorexics or bulimics sometimes do, of a heart attack due to electrolyte imbalance and malnourishment. But instead of my sin resulting in death, God was giving me life—a new life inside of me to nurture and love.

I walked through the house, astounded and filled with fear, uncertainty, and joy, and when I shared the news with David that evening, he too was overcome by God's gift to us.

Through the eyes of a mother-to-be, my entire world looked different. As the pregnancy progressed, I realized that although my life had for many years been characterized by self-destructive, self-hating, abusive patterns, this child growing inside me didn't deserve to suffer from those choices. I had not been able to overcome bulimia for my own sake, but for the love of the child within me, I was done with bulimia. My child needed a safe womb and every nutrient I could supply. I had never expected to conceive, and now that I had, I needed to do whatever it took to protect my child. That sense of awe of having a life inside me never faded.

God did not put me to shame. Instead, he was coaxing me out of my darkness into his wonderful light. David and I felt God encouraging us, pouring himself into us in ways that convinced us that our marriage—as well as our dream to make films that impact the culture for Christ—was on a path directed by him. Jesus, in ways like never before, became the Cornerstone of our lives. He had work for David and me to do. He poured out his mercy to us so we would shine the light of that mercy to others.

By December 2005, while we were expecting our child—through a marvelous series of God events that David tells about in his book *Between Heaven and Hollywood*—David joined with Russell Wolfe and Michael Scott to launch Pure Flix, which includes both a movie company to create films that reach our culture for Christ and a video-streaming source that strives to be the most trusted family-friendly source on the web. As David and our partners planned for our new venture, David and I recommitted to work hard on our marriage so that we could bring our new child into a healthy, God-honoring family.

Hidden Secrets was Pure Flix's first movie. Filming began in January 2006. There was a part I could have played, except that when the filming began, I was five months pregnant. For once, I didn't mind missing out on a role one bit. In 2006, Pure Flix released not only *Hidden Secrets*, but *The Visitation* as well.

Our biggest release of the year, however, came on June 8, 2006, with the birth of Ethan Cooper Roy.

Isn't hindsight great? As I look back on that time from our wedding day in 2003 through the watershed year of 2006, I see that, despite all our flaws and floundering, despite my own past sin and my addiction, brokenness, and helplessness, *God sustained my faith in him*. Though my understanding of God's love and character and ways was still very small, God did not see me as a burdensome disappointment who deserved his wrath. He saw me as I saw Ethan: a precious, beloved child in need of nurture, protection, and wise parenting—a child who needed to, as it says in 1 Peter 2:2, "grow up in [my] salvation."

Chapter 17

THE WAITING ROOM

This is the message we have heard from him and declare
to you: God is light; in him there is no darkness at all . . .
But if we walk in the light, as he is in the light, we have
fellowship with one another, and the blood of Jesus, his
Son, purifies us from all sin.

1 JOHN 1:5, 7

Building a spiritual house takes time—at least that's the way God goes about it with the White family. But we are living, breathing evidence that when God, the Master Builder, sets out to do so, he can transform even rubble into his dwelling place. And so, our family is home to our holy, awesome God. David and I will be the first to tell you it doesn't necessarily mean our lives are always tranquil or reverent, and certainly not predictable and orderly. It does mean every square inch of our lives—even the dark closets in our souls and the baggage packed away in hidden places, and our frolicking family room and our "grand central station" kitchen—is God's territory. The Whites belong to God—the good, the bad, the ugly, and the beautiful in all of us, and we are eternally grateful that God takes up residence in our lives.

When God chose to reveal to me that he had placed Ethan in my womb and then used that miracle as the turning point to heal me of bulimia, I understood that for me, motherhood was a sacred bond between me and God. I loved my child while he was being formed inside my body, just as God loves us when forming us in our mothers' wombs. I wanted the best for him, and I nourished my body so that it in turn could nourish his, just as God nourishes us as we grow in him. We named Ethan and loved him dearly, and in doing so I grew to understand better, as much as my human heart was capable, the magnitude of God's love for me. And that all happened before I even saw Ethan's precious little eyes or kissed his innocent face or held his tiny hand in mine. Becoming a mother expanded my grasp of God's love.

Ethan has proven himself to be a strong, energetic, happy boy, who (like his daddy) loves to chat and connect with others. He is effortlessly smart and spends hours upon hours building Legos and Minecraft. (I told him he can design my next house.) He strives to be the best in sports, and I adore watching his love for basketball flourish. And he can explain the plot of a movie better than his actress mother can! He also is a wonderful older brother to his little sisters.

GROWING PAINS

As God went about nourishing and growing us, David and I were discovering that God was doing even more than building us into a strong family; he was building our God-given mission, which also needed to go through birth pangs, stretch marks, growing pains, and complex, challenging, and rewarding experiences. Hard work, thrills, and pain, it seemed, would apply just as much to mission building as to family building.

Pure Flix was no exception. We continued to release films, but had a tumultuous series of challenges. In fact, for all of 2008 and 2009, due to a series of circumstances (several totally beyond our control), David and I had very little income, despite putting in a tremendous amount of work. Eventually we decided to sell our home and much of what we owned to ensure we would live within our means and continue to invest in our mission. To our surprise and delight, I conceived a second time and then sadly lost my second baby at ten weeks.

It was a horrific time in many ways, and it certainly wasn't easy packing up and leaving a house we loved in the wake of losing a child, or waving good-bye to financial investments we had once thought of as our safety nets.

In the process, we learned to become resourceful when it came to necessities. My best tools during our financial crisis proved to be a yellow legal pad, a pencil, and a calculator, as I learned to budget every penny and double-check every receipt. Forced to make choices about what really mattered, we discovered that our "need list" was more often a "want list," and it became easier to learn to say no to our wants.

As weeks turned to months and stretched over two years, we found we did still have everything we truly needed. We still lived in a comfortable home and always had meals on the table and clothes on our backs, even if it meant I budgeted to the penny our daily spending and allowance on a yellow note pad. Some days we even had enough to go to Baja Fresh (a nearby Mexican grill) or our favorite sushi restaurant, and some days we didn't. It certainly gave me a great appreciation for the small things and taught me to take nothing for granted.

Southern California, and the entertainment industry as a whole, is famous for its image-conscious zip codes, high-end labels, and elite retail spaces. All of this naturally leads to a subtle and demanding comparison mentality. When one is discovering how to stretch pennies, a wonderful freedom comes in being content to shop the sales at Old Navy and Target, and those great habits still serve us well today as a family of five. I truly enjoy being resourceful.

By the mercy of God and through hard lessons learned, we grew in wisdom and in confidence that God truly does provide. God's provision, however, seldom means instant, easy answers. Just as the Israelites learned when God provided manna from heaven, he wasn't snatching them *out of* the harsh and barren wilderness; he was sustaining them as they traveled *through* that painful ordeal.

One day in 2009 while preparing for Ethan's third birthday, I was picking up his birthday cake and other snacks for his party at the park that afternoon. I took the grocery cart to the checkout, only to see that my debit card had been rejected. Ethan sat in the cart with his big blue innocent eyes and the new squirt gun he wanted in his lap, and to this day I will never forget that pivotal moment. Guess what? Ethan still turned three, and we still celebrated! A friend saved the day—and yes, we did pay them back. But I will never forget that sobering moment. No harm done, except to my pride.

Perhaps the greatest gift we receive, even today, as we live through the growing pains of being built by God, is the gift of prayer, for there is nothing more precious than taking every care to our Father and learning to trust that he will meet our every need.

On February 22, 2010, Ocean Savannah Grace entered this world. I praise God that Ocean was persistent even in the womb, as I began to have preterm labor in the fifth month. My body wouldn't tolerate anti-contraction drugs, because they were causing heart problems for me, so I endured four months of strict bed rest before she arrived. Every day as I rested in bed, I trusted the goodness of God and yet also battled fears of losing my daughter. My love for her was a powerful force, and I shed many tears as I sat helplessly praying, reading, and watching Barney the Dinosaur with little Ethan in bed with me. I was allowed on my feet only to shower and use the bathroom. Daily, I begged God to keep me from going into labor too soon.

I delivered Ocean at thirty-eight weeks and praised God that she was perfect. She did, however, suffer three straight months of 24/7 colic, or more accurately, *we all* suffered through it, but we survived. She is now a delightful girly girl who loves dresses and dancing and everything pink—the epitome of a little lady! Having been a tomboy as a kid, I have enjoyed raising such a sweet, feminine-yet-feisty little girl. I love the name Ocean, because the ocean is incredibly powerful but can also be calm and peaceful. Our lovely daughter more than lives up to her name. She is also a mini-me when it comes to her wiring—fragile, empathetic, and sensitive, yet playful and goofy, with a flair for the dramatic that keeps us in stitches.

NEW PAIN MIXED WITH OLD

For Christmas 2010, my mother and her husband of sixteen years, Bob, visited us during the holidays. We had a great time. We all love Bob. He is kindhearted, like a big teddy bear. We've always thought he sort of looks like Tom Selleck. My younger brother and I had especially grown to appreciate him over the years. And he clearly adored my mother. She was his best friend.

So when I got the call in January 2011, just before Ocean turned one, I was completely shocked. Dumbfounded might be the better word. Mom had left Bob for another man. And here we go again. I was back in high school. Back to Mom's abrupt decision to leave Dad and then marry Bob a few years later. Over the years, we had never seen her and Bob fight. We hadn't even noticed any clue that anything was wrong between them. And now she was moving in with a new boyfriend.

Over the next few months, Mom and I fell back into the familiar broken relational patterns of my teen years. Mom's behavior became unpredictable and upsetting, and I responded by trying to rescue her from her choices. I genuinely wanted to help her. This response to my mom was no more helpful than it had been years ago, and just as self-defeating. Old tapes, it seemed, still played the same old broken song. The tension between us built to the point that the stress spilled over into my own emotional well-being.

Spring that year was a mix of wondrous family life mixed with painful old patterns. Watching Ethan love his baby sister brought me such joy, and I enjoyed motherhood to even greater heights. I simply loved being a mom. By contrast, the pain between my mother and me brought so many negative memories back to the surface—memories I believed to have been healed and forgiven. Spiritually, I found it confusing. But it was the beginning of an important life lesson I am still learning to this day: Healing is a process that often comes in stages—stages that cannot be rushed. New experiences can resurrect old issues thought to have been dealt with long ago. Rather than berate ourselves for not yet having been healed or not yet having fully forgiven someone, we need to recognize that a new stage of even deeper healing and forgiveness has come, and then we must step willingly into that process. But I didn't know that yet, and so I dragged guilt around with me like a heavy chain.

THE WAITING ROOM

It was during these months that I also began experiencing chronic pain throughout my body. The left side of my body would go numb, and I began having chronic migraines, which often felt as though someone had hit me with a baseball bat on my neck and spine. Crawling up the stairs by noon with exhaustion became normal. Discussions with my doctor revealed that I was suffering from fibromyalgia and thyroid issues. Could I have brought this on myself because of my years of eating disorders? There was no way to tell, and nothing to do but wait to see if it improved.

I had joined a MOPS (Mothers of Preschoolers) group when I was four months pregnant with Ocean (right before bed rest was ordered). Now the camaraderie and encouragement of other moms brought laughter into my life weekly and inspired me to see that the daily gift of mothering was making a positive, lasting investment in my two precious children.

The summer of 2011, when Ocean was a year and a half, David left for Thailand to film a movie titled *The Encounter: Paradise Lost*. He would be gone for four to six weeks while I tried to care for a five-year-old, an eighteen-month-old, and the chronic pain of my declining health. I was extremely grateful for David's nineteen-year-old niece, Alexis, who came to help me with the kids. What she couldn't help me with, however, was the strained relationship with my mom, coupled with the loneliness of feeling like a single mother raising my children while David filmed in paradise. I not only carried the weight of being a young mom with a husband away, but I (unwisely) assumed the heavy burden of attempting to rescue my own mom from her continued painful choices.

And then a botched root canal left me in horrible pain. That on top of my chronic pain left me feeling miserable. My doctor ordered an MRI—the very thought of which terrified me. I don't know what I would have done without my local MOPS group. That year at MOPS, I had become a table leader, thinking I could pour into others. It was a great comfort to step out of my own problems to engage with other mothers who shared the same craziness of parenting a preschool child. Together we shared, laughed, cried, and prayed with one another.

MOPS had assigned Melinda as my mentor mom. She was such a blessing and became a steady rock for me—a living evidence of God's presence and care in my distress. Her husband, Todd, was also going through challenging health issues, and he recommended a radiologist for my brain MRI. While I still dreaded the test, having a personal recommendation, coupled with Melinda's description of Todd's smooth MRI procedure, was reassuring.

The MRI was scheduled for nine in the evening, and I was surprised to find the medical facility nearly ready to close for the evening. David dropped me off as he was parking. The empty, dark parking lot; the lack of other patients in the eerie, shadow-filled waiting room; and the front desk tucked behind a glass window all left me feeling strangely alone. The receptionist was professional but brusque, which didn't help. I sat, shaky and afraid of the unknown. I'm so glad I didn't know this was to be my first MRI of countless more over the years.

I sat in silence in the shadowy waiting room, praying, desperately seeking comfort from God. The minutes ticked by ever so slowly. Then a woman, a hospital employee, walked through the waiting room, and the strangest thing happened. Her eyes landed on me and rested there for a moment. The next thing I knew she was walking toward me.

"Excuse me." She paused until I smiled and nodded. "I just need to tell you that you have a bright light all around you, and you're going to be okay."

I shivered at her words, and a supernatural peace swept through me, dispelling all my anxiety in an instant. God had heard my cries! He was present with me. For a moment, I simply sat there, stunned.

"Thank you so much," I said. She smiled and then turned and walked away, and I sat alone, as if nothing out of the ordinary had even occurred. But it had. Something extraordinary had taken place. God Almighty, the God who met me at the stoplight, who came to live inside me at Malibu Vineyard Church, who forgave my sins and invaded me with his Spirit, who brought me a husband before I even went looking for one, who had given me two children I never thought I'd have—that same God now reminded me that he was with me in that waiting room. God was waiting *with* me. I returned to my prayers, but they were new prayers now. Prayers of praise and thanksgiving.

God is not only God of the universe and of my family; he is God of the waiting room.

Today I'm so grateful he is, for it seems I've spent much of my life since that day in waiting rooms. I'm still learning to welcome them as sanctuaries where I can reach out for and step into the divine light that shines into our world.

TESTINGS AND BLESSINGS

In June 2012, when Ocean was two and Ethan five, I discovered I was once again expecting a child. At that time, sadly, our marriage was in a bad place. In fact, it was at its worst. I was by now one year into my medical mayhem of chronic pain—not easily managed with two small children at home. In addition to consulting doctors, I was researching everything I could get my hands on about widespread, inexplicable body pain and weakness. We were also working hard to get Pure Flix off the ground, finances were tight, hours were long, and we were bickering.

As we wrapped up the film *Revelation Road*, I was at the point of not liking who I was or who David was, and David was no happier with either of us. They say if your marriage is falling apart, the worst thing you can do is have a baby to save it. Well, God doesn't listen to earthly wisdom, and in his godly wisdom, he decided the timing was perfect for a new baby White in the world. The very thought of bringing another child into the mess that was our marriage at the time was painful. To top it off, a few days after I broke the news, David left for a week on film business.

While he was gone, I started having terrible pains on my right side, bad enough that I was doubled over. "I'm sorry," the doctor who read the ultrasound said. "The ultrasound revealed no amniotic sac in your womb, though you do have rising hormone levels consistent with pregnancy. You may have an ectopic pregnancy. This could be life threatening. You could die if your fallopian tube ruptures. You need to see your OB as soon as possible. If I were you, I'd go to the ER."

I really didn't want to go to the ER with two little ones tagging along. Since it was a Friday, "as soon as possible" to see my OB meant the following Monday. I decided to go home and try to rest until Monday.

I felt led that weekend to read *It Is Finished* by Nerida Walker, a woman who, even though she had been declared barren, was given children by God. I know we don't live in a "name it, claim it" world.

(After all, I have fought a horrific health battle for many years now.) But God led me through this weekend battle with a tenacious warrior spirit. This didn't mean I wasn't shaking in fear, pleading and begging God not to let me lose my baby. My heart, in fact, was still oozing pain from the trauma of miscarrying four years earlier, and the sadness of that loss revisited me. It seemed to be more than I could bear to have my heart broken any more than it already was. Was God there? I knew he was, because he promised to be. Because he had shown himself so many times before. Yet I was physically alone, and I *felt* alone. No one was there to reassure me, to hold my hand, to comfort me.

However, I felt a supernatural boldness in prayer and a confidence beyond explanation that I would not lose this baby. Even with my two little ones to take care of, I spent the weekend in pain and prayer. I decided to deal with this in faith, taking authority over my condition and my pain. Then, first thing on Monday, I saw my OB and had another ultrasound. The doctor explained, "We have a positive pregnancy test, and your hormone levels are consistent with pregnancy. I see an amniotic sac in your uterus, but there is no heartbeat. You could be having a miscarriage, but I think the best course of action is to treat it like an early pregnancy and hope for the best."

Here we go again, I thought. On the phone, I told David, "I can't handle it! I cannot lose another baby. I feel like I've been shattered in so many ways that I can't physically deal with another loss."

David and I were in such great emotional pain and marital discord at this point that we had little to offer to each other. But even if we couldn't find comfort in one another, I could turn to God. I spent the next two weeks pleading with God for the life of my baby. By the time of the next ultrasound, David was home and went with me. Despite my fervent prayers, I felt doomed leaving our home for the doctor's office that day. I wasn't expecting good news, because I'd certainly heard nothing like good news in my other visits. On the drive, I sat in the passenger seat crying, shaking with fear, expecting the doctor to say, "I'm sorry, but you're having a miscarriage." I had dealt with so much loss of the things I loved the most that I didn't believe I could bear this.

The same ultrasound tech I had the last time applied the jelly and moved his ultrasound wand across my belly—and there she was! A perfectly formed nine-week-old fetus, right where she should be. A miracle!

I had my miracle baby. David sat with his mouth hanging open in shock. Hallelujah! It was one of the best days of my life. And yet because David and I were on such delicate and difficult terms, he couldn't share my joy. I believe he had so prepared himself for losing the baby that he had difficulty absorbing the news. In fact, he got angry over the confusion he was feeling, and the husband I wanted to share the miracle with seemed a thousand miles away.

As with Ethan and Ocean, the miracle of another new life inside my body brightened me with a sense of awe and wonder. I do love carrying a child! Especially a child I knew was an unexpected gift of God's blessing. But that didn't change the state of our marriage. Determined to stay together, we once again sought counseling. On one visit, our discussion turned into an out-and-out shouting match.

"Is this really the kind of marriage you want to bring a new child into?" the counselor said, confronting us in the midst of our shouts. "Do you two want to separate? And what about your other two children?"

Humbled, we agreed to work at fighting *for* our marriage rather than *with* each other. Far easier said than done. But it was a turning point for us. We made the rock-solid decision that we were married for life and that our marriage and family were worth every effort we could muster. Praise God for the power of prayer and the gift of perseverance. Today, David is my very best friend, my life mate, and my partner. We are always working on our marriage, dedicated to making it grow stronger—but for us, marriage takes real work.

This pregnancy, like the one I had with Ocean, was a challenge.

I required weekly shots from a nurse to keep the little one tucked safely in my womb. But praise God, Everson Amelia Grace arrived on February 15, 2013. She gave us a scare when, a week after she was born, she didn't want to wake up. Again the panic and fear of losing her were horrifying. We rushed her to the doctor, and she recovered after some very scary moments. She is a miracle—literally! And we were more than grateful to be an intact family living together safe and sound.

Everson is a mischievous angel. With her crystal blue eyes and blonde ringlets, she makes us bend the rules when it comes to discipline. She loves to be like her big sissy and brother. And not only does she act like she rules the roost; she is also a perfect combination of a girl who loves to dance as much as she loves to play in the dirt. As she expects, she has us wrapped around her precious little finger.

It's no mistake that both daughters share the middle name of Grace, for they, like their brother, are a wonderful outpouring of God's grace in our lives.

To my surprise, God tucked a special gift into that parenthood package for me—a new experience with my mother. Shortly after each birth, Mom came to spend a week with us. After Everson's birth, watching her nurture all three of my precious children allowed me to see through new eyes her love for *me* in action. And my dad played just as important a role by being the first visitor at the hospital after each birth and sharing with us at each dedication ceremony. My gratitude as the daughter of Linda and Jim Logan grew, as did my gratitude as a daughter of God.

The thrill of parenting has been not only the greatest joy of my life but also God's means of delivering my greatest spiritual insights. In being a parent, I've come to truly understand what it means to be a child—a child of God. A child of the perfect Parent. My delight in our three children is endless, even when my every button has been pushed. They stumble and fall and stretch and grow and cry and laugh and tremble in fear and make big mistakes and small ones—and I see myself, a child of God, doing all those same things. And I see God loving me through it all. I experience the reality that nothing my children can ever do or say could make me love them any more or any less. And so it must be with God.

And yet they are children, which means they see the world from the only perspective they have—through the eyes of a child ever waiting to become a grown-up. In their world, stumbling, falling, stretching, growing, crying, laughing, making mistakes, and trembling in fear are daily occurrences. And in being a parent, those experiences are nearly daily occurrences for me as well! I've come to realize that as much as I long to be grown-up as a parent and as a faith-filled daughter of God, I'm still growing as a spiritual child.

Parents grow to understand that their children are in process, under development, not "there" yet. *Unfinished.* I would no more expect my children to be finished than I would expect a sunset without a sunrise first. Children by their very definition are on their way to becoming adults. And so it is with us! As children of God, we are on our way to becoming.

What a gift to be reminded to keep my eyes focused on what God is accomplishing rather than on the pain of getting there, not only as my children grow, but as I grow toward maturity. I am vividly aware that this is something I am *always* learning, as I certainly haven't arrived yet.

And the next few years would prove to be a powerful jump start in learning that lesson.

Chapter 18

HITTING THE BREAKS

I keep asking that the God of our Lord Jesus Christ, the glorious Father, may give you the Spirit of wisdom and revelation, so that you may know him better. I pray that the eyes of your heart may be enlightened in order that you may know the hope to which he has called you, the riches of his glorious inheritance in his holy people, and his incomparably great power for us who believe.

EPHESIANS 1:17–19

"Is she okay? What happened?" I gasped in panic, trying to hear the babysitter's voice over two-year-old Everson's bloodcurdling screams coming through the cell phone. I knew that cry—one of both fear and pain. "The car seat went flying? What do you mean?" A horrible image of my daughter, face bloodied, flashed through my mind. "Is she hurt? Didn't you have her buckled in?" I wanted to reach through the phone and hold my baby.

I turned to look for David on the soundstage where he and I, along with our cast and crew, were filming a pilot for our Pure Flix comedy television series *Hitting the Breaks*. Ironic title, under the circumstances. When I spotted him, he was already looking at me with concern. He must have heard my alarmed tone. Though we were about to roll on a new scene, he rushed toward me.

"I can explain how to reconnect the seat in a minute, but first, you need to comfort Evie until she is calmed down," I said to the babysitter. "Can you tell where she is hurt? Is there a mark? Any blood?" My voice was tense with frustration, and David was motioning for me to calm down. I was firing too many questions too quickly, but the answers weren't coming nearly quickly enough for me. I forced a deep breath as I listened to the sitter speak to Everson. I then had her put the phone to my daughter's ear so she could hear my voice. She was still crying hard. This was agony. I felt so helpless having no control over the circumstances, and I still didn't understand what had happened. I wanted to see for myself how she was, but I was more than ninety minutes away.

Evie would not calm down, but the sitter assured me there were no visible injuries. She tried to explain what happened, though not very clearly.

"I don't understand," I said. "If she was buckled in and all you did was make a normal turn in the Tahoe, how did Evie flip over?" Even asking the question frightened me. As the sitter answered, all I could picture was the look on Evie's face as her tiny body flipped and tossed about. It was agony. What if she had hit a window? Been hurled into the door headfirst? Or worse?

The director was calling for David, so I motioned to him to get back on set. Finally, I realized from the babysitter's description that when David had moved the seat to the Tahoe that morning, he must not have secured it. I talked through how to anchor it and then hung up, still shaking at Evie's continued cries and my inability to comfort her.

A (NOT SO) FUNNY THING HAPPENED ON THE WAY TO THE SITCOM

It was January 2016. David and I were in the midst of a nearly impossible schedule—filming ten sitcom episodes in only twelve weeks. We had known we would need to be away from home and at the studio four days a week, sixteen hours a day, for those twelve weeks, so we had planned that the au pair who had been with us for ten months would help care for our children in our hours away. Ethan was nine at the time, Ocean five, and Evie two. But things seldom go according to plan in the White household, and we had run into one challenge after another, not the least of which was that our au pair unexpectedly quit during the first few weeks of filming. Since then, we had been trying to get by with kind friends and short-term babysitters. This particular day—the day of the flying car seat—was a realistic example of "getting by." It was anything but smooth.

I'd love to tell you I whispered a gentle prayer of thanksgiving that my child was now safe and then elegantly drifted back to my place on set. But of course, that would be a lie. I felt as if my heart rate had tripled. It is stunning how many frightening thoughts can flit through your mind in a matter of seconds. I envisioned an ambulance with EMTs standing by and a social worker reprimanding us for being absent-minded parents with overbooked schedules. But most of all, I kept picturing my youngest hurtling like a missile toward the windshield. I couldn't decide which I needed more at the moment—a good cry in the dressing room or a scream of frustration in a sound booth. But neither was an option.

"Andrea, I need you at your mark," the second assistant director announced, and within moments, with a big smile as if I didn't have a care in the world, I was acting my comedic role. And that is why we call it acting: I was not smiling on the inside! In truth, I had many cares weighing on me, but I had no other choice but to keep them tucked deeply inside. I didn't want to look frazzled. I wanted to appear totally in control, relaxed, confident, and in the moment.

Hours later, with the day's shooting done, I dragged myself back to the wardrobe and makeup room. I checked the well-lit makeup mirror to see if the bizarre rash on my face was still hidden beneath my makeup but found it was not. Thank God for camera filters! My skin never breaks out, but on this week of shooting, it had erupted—an actor's nightmare. Cameras can be brutal in showing flaws. But I had no time to take off the heavy makeup from the shoot, no matter how much my skin bothered me. It was already 9:00 p.m., and I still had a ninety-minute drive to get home so I could relieve the sitter and kiss my (hopefully) sleeping children. The stress of this schedule had been crazy, and it wasn't over. We had weeks to go, with no letup.

I questioned again our sanity for planning such an accelerated shoot, with rehearsals every Thursday and filming every Friday, Saturday, and Sunday, all from 8:00 a.m. to 9:00 p.m., with a ninety-minute drive on both ends. That left Monday through Wednesday at home to study the week's script while trying to squeeze in all the duties of being a mama and running a household.

Generally, David is the workhorse who keeps the Pure Flix ball spinning. In contrast, I love a flexible mix of working and raising a family. My children have always come first, and thankfully I have managed to work as an actor and keep my children first. Acting and being creative make my spirit leap with excitement, and I love the freedom of stepping out of the reality of my own life to explore a character. By nature, I am an introvert and am happy in my little world, so when opportunities come, I appreciate getting out of my comfort zone and doing what I love to do—act.

Creating a sitcom was something we had looked forward to for a long while, and now that the time was upon us, we knew we needed to jump at it. When opportunities knock in this business, you open the door and just do what you must do. They don't often knock twice. While the success of *God's Not Dead* had improved our financial situation considerably, like most performers, David and I desire to work consistently.

Still, I confess I was feeling the weight of having had to kiss my three little ones good-bye at 6:30 for the fourth day in a row, and I was struggling with the guilt of knowing they'd be sound asleep when I finally got home at 10:30 at night. Just that very morning, Evie had wrapped her little arms around my neck and begged me to stay home with her. I hurt at the memory, especially considering the car accident that day. But mama guilt and fatigue were not my only struggles.

NO LAUGHING MATTER

Five long, hard years of serious health issues, from 2011 to 2016, with all the emotional and spiritual baggage that go along with it, had worn me down. The enemy had been battling hard to *steal and kill and destroy* my life. Despite medical professionals; an endless list of treatments, diagnoses, supplements, and therapies; the prayers of many; and the power of God's Word, the battle raged on. The symptoms and the fear that came along with them had been making my life smaller and smaller as the enemy claimed territory—killing my joy, stealing my hope, and trying desperately to destroy my faith. There is no question that the combination of yet unhealed hurts from my past, my perfectionism, and the lack of control over my broken body had escalated to a spiritual crisis as agonizing as my battles with anorexia and bulimia.

As of yet, I saw no miracle in sight. The doctors with whom I had consulted during that time diagnosed me with any number of things:

- acute debilitating migraines
- chronic fatigue syndrome
- fibromyalgia (a disorder characterized by widespread musculoskeletal pain accompanied by fatigue, sleep, memory, and mood issues)
- hypothyroidism
- Lyme disease and co-infections
- porphyria (a group of disorders that result from a buildup of natural chemicals that produce porphyrin in one's body, mainly affecting the nervous system, skin, and other organs)

- POTS, also known as postural tachycardia syndrome (a condition in which changing to an upright position causes an abnormal increase in heart rate)
- premature ventricular contractions (PVCs), which are extra, abnormal heartbeats that begin in one of the heart's two lower pumping chambers

If you are familiar with even a few of these, you probably know that of the complex series of symptoms these conditions exhibit, several are true of more than one condition, making it extremely difficult to know where one begins and the other ends, what treatments to pursue, and whether I am experiencing a short-term symptom or a serious threat requiring immediate medical attention. We have invested enormous amounts of time and money into doctors, alternative practitioners, Lyme disease specialists, a neurologist, a cardiologist, an herbalist, and an endocrinologist; lab work; and visits to the ER.

During the editing of this book, I've gotten some additional news. An abnormal EEG resulted in a diagnosis of epileptiform abnormalities, for which I've been prescribed seizure medication. My doctors have diagnosed me with so many conditions and prescribed so many medications, that at this point there are many I haven't taken because of my lack of peace and a scary list of side effects. I am praying for peace and wisdom to know what to take and what not to take. Sometimes we don't know what to do, but we have to trust God and rely on his Holy Spirit for help. The unknowns keep me in a state of childlike faith, and now I must simply rest in the trust that God knows I am beautifully broken and that he will complete his healing in his perfect timing.

Physically, my life is painful, and my daily activities are severely hindered. I still pack lunches, make breakfast, and try to do all the mom duties without complaining. But most of my friends and family don't see the side of me that takes three days to recover after one busy day. Or the tears that come from a three-day migraine. Or the days I can't take my daughter to dance because I'm hanging by a thread. I hate to admit that. I show up when I can, and when my mommy friends say, "How are you? I haven't seen you in so long," I just smile and say, "Great to see you!" I try not to talk about how things are going; I usually change the subject. Being an actor comes in handy—I can force a smile and pretend it's all good.

But the effects go well beyond the physical. The spiritual and psychological tolls are significant as well. God says he never leaves us or forsakes us, but I have never felt so alone, afraid, and defeated as I have in the relentless storm of medical issues. While sitting in waiting rooms, I try to remember the phenomenal experience of the woman who told me of the light surrounding me—a powerful memory that calls me from an earthbound to an eternal perspective. But I confess, it takes lots of work, and more times than not, I still feel alone. It is then that I must rely on truth, not feelings.

Because I frequently experience a sudden, unpredictable onset of severe symptoms, anxiety has become a major issue, often leaving me trapped in fight-or-flight mode. And I discovered as symptom after symptom invaded my body that many unresolved childhood issues resurfaced. The weakness I felt as a child was triggered when I felt weak; the sense of loss and betrayal I felt as a child loomed large again as I lost function and felt betrayed by my body; unresolved anger surfaced, and I felt alone in facing my fears; and finally, as any perfectionist will understand, my desire for control over the uncontrollable heightened.

BACK TO THE SITCOM

Forty-five minutes after leaving the set, I sat at a near standstill on the 101 freeway, the rhythm of the wipers accompanying the rapid patter of raindrops on the roof of my Tahoe.

"Ugh, you've got to be kidding me. A traffic jam on a Sunday night?"

I muttered. "Why on an evening when we went late? On the day when Evie's car seat flipped? When I just want to get home to cuddle my babies?" A flood of tears began to drip down my cheeks.

"Lord, why is all of this happening now, of all times? First Ethan's illness last week just when I was having my head-bashing migraines, and then these horrid skin issues and the fever on Tuesday and barely being able to walk yesterday—and yet I have to appear at the soundstage like I have it all together and my life is flawless." I know this might have sounded like an angry rant, but it wasn't. It was the desperate heart cry of a woman who felt she had reached the end of her rope and found herself dangling over an abyss of years of unanswered prayers.

"O God, I'm sorry for being angry, but I'm weary and discouraged. I think you've mistaken me for someone else. I am not as strong as you must think. I'm hanging by a thread. It has been just one bad thing after another, and it makes me wonder if you're punishing me for something. Is that it? Or is it the enemy, trying to steal my joy and distract me from living for you? I can't escape the feeling that I'm being punched and punched and punched again and then kicked in the face when I'm down. I struggle to find joy—and often don't find it at all when symptoms land me in bed and unable to function. How can I possibly overcome these trials? I know, God, you've heard it all before. You have given us so much and you haven't caused this, but you've continued to allow this."

I stopped crying and calmed myself. *The enemy is so good at whispering all the things that are wrong with us and our lives,* I thought. *And Hollywood is great at reminding me of everything I am not. God and his Word are the only things that tell me what we ARE. God's Word is true and life-giving.*

The traffic flow picked up, and soon I was back up to the speed limit. *Good. I might make it home not much later than 10:30 after all.* It would be a relief to get at least five hours of sleep tonight. Tomorrow was Monday, and I could be with Ethan, Ocean, and Everson nearly all day. I'd take them with me to my doctor appointment. (My sixth in three weeks. Don't ask!) Monday, Tuesday, and Wednesday would require no studio time. Yay! I could study my lines for Thursday, but still take my time playing my favorite role—mama to our kids.

I know that some moms dread the daily tasks of making breakfast, checking homework, and getting their kiddos ready for school. I relish it. My heart sings as I look for ways to make it playful and fun, showing them in concrete ways that they matter to me, that they are loved and enjoyed—the very messages I longed for when I was a child.

Focusing on my kids had calmed me.

That's the answer, I told myself. *Just focus on all the good things.*

So I did. David and I were thrilled with our lineup of special guest stars. I was excited to be working with Reginald VelJohnson this week, who had worked with us on handful of our other films. I had been watching his warm, expressive face since I was a child tuning in to *Family Matters*. The following week—Morgan Fairchild. It would be my first time to work with her. To me, she was a legend—an eighties icon whom I watched as I was growing up. She and Ray Wise played my parents in the sitcom. He also has been in several of our Pure Flix films, like *Brother White*, *Revelation Road*, and *God's Not Dead 2*. A joy to work with. And Tim Tebow, the former NFL football player now baseball player, whose faith is bright and bold in the midst of criticism. It would be fun to work with him in his upcoming guest appearance.

My emotions had calmed considerably, so I listed more positives. I thought of David's excitement that Burt Reynolds was part of *Hitting the Breaks*. He worked with Burt in his very first acting job when he arrived in L.A.—in Burt's hit series *Evening Shade*. Burt had encouraged David greatly by expanding David's role in that series, so it was special to have Burt doing the voiceover in *Hitting the Breaks*. He played the deceased father of David's character, who narrates the series and ties up the end of each episode with an inspiring takeaway. And to top it all off, it was a great joy, despite the stress, to be creating a show that an entire family can enjoy together—a deep passion for us at Pure Flix.

The positive thoughts were flowing now.

Then I caught sight of my left eye in the mirror and did a double take. It was drooping—as if the muscles of the lid and the area around it had gone lax. "My eye!" I cried. "What's going on with my eye?" The familiar feeling of panic rose from deep in my chest, and for the second time in a day, I had to take deep breaths to calm myself. *Note to self,* I thought. *Add this to the list of symptoms to discuss with the doctors this week.*

KEEP ASKING

All in all, this isn't a pretty picture of me, is it?

I felt like I was living a bad joke. Not that my list of trials is funny. On the days we weren't shooting, I had mostly been running, kids in tow, from one medical specialist to another—getting MRIs and CT scans and countless blood draws—all in an attempt to understand my crazy list of scary, mysterious symptoms. But each diagnosis seemed worse than the one before. And . . . well, you get the picture.

No. It wasn't *funny* in the sense of the warm laughter of a family sitcom. But ironic? Yes, it was funny in that way. Even more ironic was that all of these things had been happening just as David and I were finally enjoying the fruit of many years of labor. God had been opening so many doors over the past few months. As we were filming the sitcom, emails and letters were still coming in from all over the globe, filled with stories of faith stirred and lives changed from our recent film *God's Not Dead*. David was receiving many invitations to speak at events that just months before wouldn't have given him the time of day—people who, before the film, refused our calls and scoffed at us as "those people making little Christian films." And financially, the success of the movie was providing resources us like never before to realize the dreams we had for our mission to reach our culture for Jesus.

God's Not Dead had been declared by Nash Information Services as the sixth most profitable movie in film industry history (based on percentage return on investment), just behind number five, *Grease* (1978), and just before number seven, *Star Wars: A New Hope* (1977).* Executives in the entertainment industry were still trying to wipe the stunned looks off their faces! Pure Flix had gone overnight from a laughingstock in some circles to the sought-after interview of the week. Now *that* was funny!

"What was the secret of your success?"

"What was your strategy?"

"What's your next move?"

All the interviewers were asking those same questions. I loved how David answered them: "We have no secret. We simply did just what we have been doing at Pure Flix all along—we made a film that uplifts and inspires the human spirit. We are creating movies with the purpose of changing our culture for Christ, one film at a time. And that's what we are going to continue to do."

Despite the deep flaws in my faith and my self-condemnation, there was no question that God had given me, in this unique moment in time, a platform—a loudspeaker to our culture—powerful enough to reach the ears of many people in our world who either don't know him at all or do know him but struggle as I do to know him better. Which is yet another reason I feel called to press on, even though my body often cries, "Stop!"

The irony of the timing of all the accolades, all the influence, all the resources, all the suffering, and all the doubts and questions seemed perfectly capped off by the fact that, quite naturally, Pure Flix has a dedicated social media effort. When I look at how we appear in social

---

* "The Numbers: Movie Budget and Financial Performance Records: Most Profitable Movies, Based on Return on Investment," *Nash Information Services*, © 1997–2016. Alll rights reserved, www .the-numbers.com/movie/budgets (accessed February 22, 2017).

media, I have to tell you, it sometimes makes me feel like a fraud. In social media, it looks like the Whites are living the dream 24/7 and have life all figured out. *This is so far from the truth!*

In a nutshell, here I was, sixteen years since becoming a believer in Jesus, and I was still struggling, trying to figure out the differences between God's discipline, the enemy's attacks, my own responsibility for what was going wrong, the privilege of suffering for the gospel, and the inevitable suffering we all experience from living in a fallen world where painful toil is our lot in life. Surely, I could not be the only one struggling to tell the difference. And being the perfectionist I am, my responses to all my troubles—no matter their reason—were falling miserably short of what I wanted my response to be.

This is exactly where I was as I began writing this book.

Life is hard! Every one of us is walking through one kind of a storm or another. The reality is, the storms don't end and life doesn't get easy, and though our trials may end, it may take years to see God's hand in them. Then new trials arise. One step at a time, one day at a time, we choose to keep our eyes fixed on Jesus and his perfect work. Not consumed by our expectations of a perfect life, but opening ourselves to a life forever being sharpened, refined, and pruned. For God's glory and by his grace, we keep walking.

Which is why I chose the verses at the beginning of this chapter. Go back and read them again, taking special note of the first three words: *I keep asking.* Yes, we must *keep* asking. The recurring questions that come while living an unfinished life are never simply answered once and for all. We are not finished yet. We are not perfected yet. God, the pioneer and perfecter of our faith, is the one who is going about perfecting us, and he uses a lifetime on this earth to prepare us for eternity with him. Some questions will not be answered until we meet him face-to-face.

So, as a little child of the Father, I will never stop seeking his Spirit of wisdom and revelation. I will never cease stretching to know him better. I will continue to storm the gates of heaven, asking that the eyes of my heart may be enlightened, so that I may know the hope to which he has called me, because God has for us, in our completion, a glorious inheritance and his incomparably great power. For *us*. For his dearly loved children who believe in him.

I don't know about you, but I've decided I don't ever want to pretend I have the answers to these immense questions. In those verses, I hear an open invitation from God to keep on asking and asking and asking.

Chapter 19

THE BEAUTY
OF BROKEN

Now the Lord is the Spirit, and where the Spirit of the
Lord is, there is freedom. And we all, who with unveiled
faces contemplate the Lord's glory, are being transformed
into his image with ever-increasing glory, which comes
from the Lord, who is the Spirit.

2 CORINTHIANS 3:17–18

David pulled over to the curb at the Los Angeles International Airport
and dropped me off, along with Ethan (now ten), Ocean (six), and our pile
of luggage, so the three of us could check in for our flight. Meanwhile, he
and Everson (three) went to park our car. After divvying up our suitcases
and carry-ons among the three of us, I awkwardly maneuvered my two
kiddos and the luggage through the pressing crowds to the ticket counter.

"Mommy, I don't want to leave without them," Ocean said anxiously.

"We won't, sweetie. Daddy and Evie are just parking the car. They
will meet us at the ticket counter."

This was our first family vacation since Everson had been born. All
three children had flown with me when I filmed *Mom's Night Out*, but
that was nearly three years ago, so they were pretty green when it came
to flying. We originally had this trip planned for June, but due to my

illnesses, we had to postpone it, just as we had other family vacations the past few years. Our anticipation had been building all summer, and now, in mid-August 2016, we were finally on our way. The children were vibrating with excitement. This wouldn't be just a little puddle jump of an hour or so, but a five-hour flight to Hawaii.

Soon we were all together, snaking our way through the hot, over-crowded security line. David and I were doing our best to shepherd the kids through the security process with as little anxiety as possible. How eye-opening to see it through the eyes of a child. Both Ocean and Evie feared that the conveyer belt was stealing their things. Despite our assurances, their faces showed visible relief when they were reunited with their carefully packed carry-ons. And how about that huge walk-through metal detector? None of them were fond of passing through that alone with no hand to hold.

How ironic. The very thing designed to keep them safe was the object of their fears. How like us as children in our faith. The very experiences designed to mature and prepare us for what lies ahead are the very experiences we fear. I didn't miss the irony—as I was calming their fears, I was reaching for God to calm my own.

During my last two flights (the most recent of which was nearly two years before this day), I'd had very frightening, horrendous physical symptoms: wild fluctuations in blood pressure, heart palpitations, acute migraines, and difficulty breathing. I had even blacked out and lost my vision for a short time. I literally felt as though I was dying. Some might be tempted to attribute my symptoms to anxiety. If so, they should keep that opinion to themselves. While it's true that anxiety no doubt played a role in my problems on those flights, it's also true that I was by now in my fifth year of my ordeal with diagnosed health conditions. How might those health issues have contributed to my reactions on those other flights? Might the same thing happen today? I had no answers to those questions.

That's why, as we prepared for this day, I had consulted with two of my doctors and had been given the all clear to fly. One of them had told me I could take a portable oxygen unit along if it would reassure me, but I declined. If all these other people could fly without oxygen, then in faith I was determined to do it too.

My Fitbit told me my heart rate was well over 120 just standing, and I could feel stress physically pummeling me. The uncertainty over how my body, especially my blood pressure, would respond to the plane ride had me worked up. Knowing I had to increase my pressure before liftoff, I drank some Gatorade—which I also used to take my prescribed steroids.

Spiritually, determined that I would get onto the plane, I'd been doing some intense preparation for a few weeks by meditating on Scripture and praying. I knew from experience that with God, I am never alone, yet when my symptoms are severe, it is an intensely lonely experience. I would need God's help to remain calm. One verse in particular had spoken to me about my choice to make this trip: "I have set before you life and death, blessings and curses. Now choose life, so that you and your children may live and that you may love the LORD your God, listen to his voice, and hold fast to him" (Deuteronomy 30:19–20). I was determined to choose life, to fully live it with my children, and to hold fast to God. I believed he wanted me with my family for this trip, even if my body was telling me otherwise—and it certainly was! Another verse gave me courage as the trip approached: "Therefore my heart is glad and my tongue rejoices; my body also will rest secure" (Psalm 16:9).

But to be perfectly honest, as I approached the boarding gate that day, it was a real challenge to *hold fast* and *rest secure*. I was afraid! During those harried moments, there were too many questions and distractions from the kids to thoughtfully meditate on those Scriptures. Determined that my tongue would rejoice, I silently prayed over and over, *Thank you, Lord, that "I can do all things through Christ who strengthens me"* (Philippians 4:13 NKJV).

DOING BATTLE

For months now, I fully realized I was battling not just physical issues but also spiritual forces for this family trip. God had used my past to instill in me tenacity and perseverance. I called on those qualities now. And not just for this trip. I was doing battle with those same forces for my health overall. I had made it an all-out battle campaign. Physical battle. Intellectual battle. Spiritual battle. Physically, I was still seeing my specialists, following their orders, participating in treatments, lab tests, and diagnostic tests as they recommended. Intellectually, I was researching every bit of medical and professional wisdom I could lay my hands on and pursuing the most appropriate and promising treatments. *And above all*, I thought as we boarded the plane, took our seats, and buckled up, *I am doing battle for my faith.*

God says he never leaves us or forsakes us, but I have never felt so alone, forsaken, afraid, and defeated as I have in the relentless storm of medical issues, each one a brutal reminder that I completely lack control over my body and its malfunctions. So, for week after week, month after month, for five long years, I had endured the piling up of one struggle after another and one health crisis after another to the point that the perfectionist in me was plagued with a long list of embarrassing questions. Questions I've continued to struggle with even as I've been writing this book:

- Again, Lord, really? More suffering?
- Haven't I learned enough yet to live in victory?
- Why can't I overcome this?
- Why is God not overcoming this for me?
- Is God allowing this suffering and these complications because I'm being punished?
- Does God not really love me?

- Did God not say we are more than conquerors in Christ Jesus?
  Then why hasn't this been conquered?
- God, am I disappointed in you or in me? (That one, I realized
  with a heavy heart, I did know the answer to: *Both.* I did not like
  that answer!)

I was weary from my incessant questions that rattled my confidence
in God and my relationship with him. I was also ashamed of many of
them, given the fact that God had proven himself present and faithful
in so many aspects of my life. After all, how could I doubt the God who
had spoken to me at a stoplight, saved me from my sins, delivered me
twice from bulimia, gifted us with three children who all are growing
healthy and strong, saved our marriage, enabled us to launch Pure Flix,
and was now prospering it?

Who was I to doubt such a God? Yet I had to admit I was angry
with God because I couldn't find the answers to my questions. In truth,
I was a mess. My body was broken. My spirit was in shreds. My soul was
scarred with self-condemnation, asking how much of this had I brought
on myself as that champion of self-destruction who starved and abused
her body in all the years of anorexia and bulimia. There was no way to
answer that question.

I thought I would have grown more by now. I thought my faith had
matured more. I thought my trust ran deeper. But I seemed to come back,
over and over, to the same spot. I felt forsaken. I had reached the point of
realizing that every new traumatizing experience was adding another scar
on my soul. I was so frustrated at times that I didn't know if I wanted to
run toward God or away from him.

But that's not how I want to live! That would be allowing the enemy
to win. And even with those scary questions, even with the apparent
lack of answers, God's Spirit within me was still telling me I would be
victorious. I didn't know how or when that victory would come, but

I would not run away. Instead, I would turn and fight. I would fight for my faith, just as years ago David and I had determined to fight for our marriage—relentlessly.

It seemed to me I'd been fighting my entire life, even though at times I fought for the wrong things. I fought the destructive labels of my childhood and the broken identity they produced, the effects of a broken family and the reputation I feared, the battle of control over my body—manifested in anorexia—and the doubters and naysayers that declared I'd never be an actor. I'd also fought for an acting career through all the tough dead ends.

They were not all healthy battles, nor had I won them all. But I had fought them, even if I emerged battered and bloody at the end. Somewhere between my being a landing pad for an ATV and deciding to become an actor, God had given me a fighter's heart. If I could fight all of those battles before I even knew the Lord, I was determined I would never stop fighting for my faith to grow stronger.

And I had fought battles after coming to faith as well. I'd fought painful distractions along the way. I'd fought the false security I'd once looked for in men and fought to be pure and celibate once I had come to the Lord. I'd fought for each pregnancy, for my marriage, for Pure Flix, for my family.

Now I was fighting the enemy as I climbed aboard that plane on our way to a family vacation in Hawaii. I refused to allow him to make my *life* smaller; I refused to allow the enemy to make my *faith* smaller. But I knew I couldn't fight this battle alone. I needed battle advice from God Almighty.

And I found it in 2 Corinthians.

TAKING CAPTIVES

The apostle Paul writes this to the believers in Corinth and to us today:

> For though we live in the world, we do not wage war as the world
> does. The weapons we fight with are not the weapons of the world.

On the contrary, they have divine power to demolish strongholds.
We demolish arguments and every pretension that sets itself up
against the knowledge of God, and we take captive every thought
to make it obedient to Christ.

2 CORINTHIANS 10:3–5

God says to take captives! And not just any captives, but those enemies that set themselves up against the knowledge of God. Who would
have predicted God would single out for capture these enemies? *Our
own thoughts.* We are to capture our thoughts and make them obedient
to Jesus Christ.

I so get this! I get it because it was my thought-life that was attacking
my faith, and I knew it. I just didn't know how to break the power of my
thoughts. But God tells us how in this powerful battle strategy: "Do not
conform to the pattern of this world, but be transformed by the renewing
of your mind. Then you will be able to test and approve what God's will
is—his good, pleasing and perfect will" (Romans 12:2).

We can search out our thoughts that are enemies of our faith, and
take away their freedom to wield their influence over us. Then we must
subject them to Jesus' authority—which is found in only one place—the
Word of God. By filling our minds with the Word of God that corrects
our wrong thinking, our minds will be renewed with the truth, and that
truth will transform it.

For my own sake, I need to break it down to the simplest language:
Armed with the truth of God's Word, confront my own destructive
thoughts that are attacking my faith. Force those wrong thoughts to
surrender to God's truth.

To do this for my trip to Hawaii, I needed to choose a section of
Scripture that got right to the heart of my issue. That was easy for me to
figure out—my issue was brokenness. Physical, spiritual, and emotional
brokenness. I was sick and tired of being broken and feeling broken.

And so I found a portion of the New Testament that was a 100 percent challenge to the way I was thinking about brokenness. I'll tell you now, it was a like a fresh wind that—pardon the pun—blew my view of brokenness to pieces. *It celebrates brokenness!*

JARS OF CLAY

Let me warn you that this is rather long section of Scripture, so I'm going to break it up. I'm going to quote from part of 2 Corinthians 4. It will be tempting to skim over it, telling yourself you've read it before. Resist the temptation, and stick with me here. See if this transforms your thinking the way it has transformed mine.

> For God, who said, "Let light shine out of darkness," made his light shine in our hearts to give us the light of the knowledge of God's glory displayed in the face of Christ.
>
> 2 CORINTHIANS 4:6

So far so good. Most of us already understand the idea that God's light shines in our hearts. But take a look at the next verse with this question in mind: Where does God place this light of the knowledge of his glory?

> But we have this treasure in jars of clay to show that this all-surpassing power is from God and not from us.
>
> 2 CORINTHIANS 4:7

God places his light in nothing more than mere jars of clay—everyday earthen vessels. That would be us. We're made of dirt. His awesome power that surpasses every other power in heaven and earth is placed in mere humans. I can think of a few people who brought the light to me in dark times. Mattie's mom, who offered prayers at the kitchen table. The two policemen who stayed by my side when I overdosed on cocaine. The stranger in the car at the intersection who urged me to flip my radio dial to a certain station. Amazing jars of clay! But jars of clay are temporary, common, and breakable. Clay doesn't stand the test of time on this earth. It ages, just as we age. It crumbles, just as we crumble. It cracks.

What was God thinking? Why not place his precious message, his treasure of light and power, inside the angels, who are heavenly beings? Why in us, those who are in mere mortal bodies? Why in me, with my body that is broken and crumbling and hurting every day, flawed and weak?

It gets even more mysterious. Even though our human bodies are but clay, once we are filled with the light of Christ, something amazing happens.

> We are hard pressed on every side, but not crushed; perplexed, but not in despair; persecuted, but not abandoned; struck down, but not destroyed.
>
> 2 CORINTHIANS 6:8–9

This is a very big idea packed into very few words. When bad things happen, the light and power inside of us are not destroyed. Nothing can damage God's power that lives in our spirits. Our clay bodies may get damaged, but God's power that lives in us cannot be destroyed. Why?

> We always carry around in our body the death of Jesus, so that the life of Jesus may also be revealed in our body. For we who are alive are always being given over to death for Jesus' sake, so that his life may also be revealed in our mortal body.
>
> 2 CORINTHIANS 6:10–11

While our flawed, imperfect, temporary, sin-natured old selves in clay vessels are wasting away, inside we are being renewed over and over, more and more, to the ever-increasing glory of God. His light that overcomes darkness is revealed through us when we serve God.

And now comes the glorious part—the final reward that helps us understand that these clay vessels were never meant to last:

> Therefore we do not lose heart. Though outwardly we are wasting away, yet inwardly we are being renewed day by day. For our light and momentary troubles are achieving for us an eternal glory that far outweighs them all.
>
> 2 CORINTHIANS 6:16–17

Eternal wins! Temporary loses! And our troubles, from an eternal perspective, are only *momentary*. Yet those troubles of ours can accomplish something great! (Reread that sentence.) As our troubles reveal our weaknesses, God's light comes pouring out of the cracks and crevices of our broken places. God's power inside us is being renewed; his light is growing; and he is transforming us into eternal beings who reflect his glory.

> So we fix our eyes not on what is seen, but on what is unseen, since what is seen is temporary, but what is unseen is eternal.
>
> 2 CORINTHIANS 6:18

We can choose to keep our attention, our focus, on the eternal power and glory of God. That is what lasts. That is what matters. That is what we live for. To carry it, embody it, grow in it, and shine it.

WHAT IF?

This mystery—Christ in us, though we are mere jars of clay—resonates strongly with me. When bulimia was ravaging my life and I was afraid I was dying, yet helpless to stop it, God placed the life of Ethan inside me.

Instantly, my urge to binge and purge ended because I had a purpose far above my own life. I had a new life inside me. I lived to give life to that life.

So it is with the life of Jesus, the Light of the world inside us. We can choose to live to nurture that life, that transformation, that freedom, inside us. When I was pregnant with Ocean and thought her life had died within me, I grieved, but then—miracle of miracles—she had not died at all. She lived inside me. My heart leaped, for where I had thought there was death, there was life. My energy and efforts went into preparing a stronger family to welcome her into, one that would nourish her and help her grow.

And when our marriage was near death, God planted the life of Everson inside me, and that life brought new life into our marriage. The enemy wrapped his manipulative fingers around our marriage, threatening to choke the life out of our union, yet God delivered Everson's life and our marriage through it all.

As a woman who has lived now for some years with daily, painful reminders that my body is weak and broken, the reality that even in my weakness I can carry life inside me is nothing short of a miracle. The same is true for all of us. It is nothing short of a miracle that the Light of the world has taken up residence inside us. We have a choice to make. What will we do with this gift? Will we ignore it and scorn it? Or will we nurture it, enjoy it, celebrate it, protect it, and eagerly anticipate how God will renew us through it day by day?

How could we not?

His life inside of us is what matters above all else, because not only will he never die or fade away; he is transforming us more and more into his perfect image in preparation for our freedom from the brokenness of this earth.

Are you willing to consider a rather scary question—one with all kinds of complex theological implications?

What if the Light of the world, who loves us more than we can fathom, is actually at work to deliberately push on all those cracks in our temporary, fragile jars of clay—all of our raw, tender, oozing, torn-up, ragged, deeply painful cracks—until he finds a way to let them split us wide open so God's light can pour into us and through us and out to others?

I love that image!

It gives purpose and power and benefit for the painful breaking—it transforms brokenness into beautiful light!

This is the beauty of broken! Our focus is on opening ourselves up to the light of Jesus growing inside us.

Every crack is a reminder of the work God is doing.

Every broken place is a place of anticipation of how God is transforming us.

Every fracture is a place that reminds us we have an eternal inheritance ahead of us—to that time when we will live face-to-face with the God of all-surpassing love.

Every time we come to the edge of our trust, instead of berating our failure to trust God for that next scary step, we hear the voice of our Lord, saying, "Wonderful. See that step you are afraid to take today? That's the next territory I'm preparing you to conquer."

I confess I'm afraid of volunteering to live a broken, poured-out life, because being broken is painful, and dying to self is, well, how do I put this? *Dying to self means you're dead.* It just isn't in *my* best interest, right?

Only until I look at the alternative. What would I rather do? Choose me over Jesus? A quick reread of chapters 4–10 reveals exactly where those kinds of decisions took me. It sent me, as it would send you, wandering through dark rooms in hopeless mansions. It drives us down roads that lead only to dead ends.

Either way, I get broken. Willingly broken to beam more light to others, or pointlessly broken by my own sinful choices. Either way, I am just a jar of clay. This body is made of the dust of the earth, and to dust it will return. The broken spirit within me, if not broken for Christ, is broken and dying from sin.

So I'm going to take the long view of the transformation of my soul until I stand in the presence of God Almighty, pure and blameless and beyond reproach. I'm going to focus on the light I have and fix my eyes on Jesus. I am going to see my present as one step that leads me closer to my completion in Christ.

Lord, I want to live beautifully broken!

JUST SHOW UP

As the jet took off from LAX on that August day in 2016, I didn't fly delivered; I flew broken. When I felt lightheaded, I spoke the words of life from Scripture. I did my best to focus on the eternal, unseen view. I reminded myself that even if I did black out, others would care for me. I stared down my fear of death eye to eye and decided that if I were to die, I'd be in God's glorious light that much sooner. When a splitting migraine did take hold, I reminded myself how temporary it was—and that at least it hit on my way to a beautiful place with my family rather than at home alone.

I didn't have to show up for my family vacation in a healthy, vibrant, energetic body; I just had to *show up*.

The entire time, I kept in mind that three little sets of eyes were watching how I faced my fears and pain. I wanted them to see that we are more than conquerors in Christ Jesus, even when it means we cannot conquer bad things *before* they happen to us, but that instead we can endure hardship with confidence in God's help. I wanted them to see my eyes focused on the unseen, not on the seen.

This imperfect mother spent a week with my imperfect family living beautifully broken on the lovely island of Hawaii. We quarreled, got food poisoning, got grumpy, and snapped at one another in some very long lines. We also laughed, marveled at the beauty of the place, shared the somber reverence of Pearl Harbor, wiggled our toes in the sand, and played in the foaming waves. Every day my body hurt—every trying, tiring, precious, wonderful, eternally significant day.

And while I went about my fight each day, God did what God does. He shined his light through my cracks.

One of those days, we stopped at Target to stock up on water, and David and I got into a spat in one of the aisles. (Probably because we'd been there three times in four days!) A family approached us and said to David, "Weren't you in the movie *God's Not Dead*?" A wonderful conversation followed that reminded us that God is using that movie, and others too, to bring eternity into the minds of people all over the globe.

On the day we visited Pearl Harbor, three young men in their twenties came over to us, eager to talk with David about their thoughts after seeing *God's Not Dead*. How exciting to hear them grapple with God's truth! As they walked away, excited that God had brought them into contact with David, I wondered how God would use each of them in his service in his world.

Another day, we grabbed a meal at Subway on the way to the beach. David was ordering sandwiches while I was scolding Ethan, explaining why he couldn't have orange soda. (Sorry, Ethan! Mama knows best.) A precious woman approached me. "Excuse me, but are you the Whites? The ones who make Christian movies?" she asked. As we chatted, she said, "My husband is in the military. Sometimes people thank him for his service to our country. I just want to thank you for your service to the Lord."

Can you believe how good and faithful God is? Despite our flaws, failings, and human frailty, he uses us, beautifully broken, everywhere we go.

I think the most powerful discovery for me in embracing my beautifully broken life is that while I cannot control the symptoms of my illnesses or my circumstances or the chaos of this crazy world, I can control my choices.

I can just show up to be used by God.

I can choose to stop pleading with God to answer the *why* and *when* questions. He is an eternal God with eternal *why* and *when* reasons that are far beyond my field of vision. Instead, I can ask God the *what* and *how* and *who* questions. I can pray like this:

Dear Lord,
What would you have me to do in this circumstance?
How do I show your love in this messy world?
Who would you have me reach out to today?
What would you have me say?
How would you have me act?
Who needs to hear from me that they matter in this world?

I can choose to live out my purpose in this world. I can choose to rely on his power to carry out that purpose. I can choose to look forward every single day to being transformed more and more into the image of Christ with ever-increasing glory. And I can anticipate my eternal reward of living in complete freedom, perfected in Jesus Christ.

I gladly choose to live in the beauty of broken.

Chapter 20

PERFECTLY UNFINISHED

I pray that out of his glorious riches he may strengthen you
with power through his Spirit in your inner being, so that
Christ may dwell in your hearts through faith. And I pray
that you, being rooted and established in love, may have
power, together with all the Lord's holy people, to grasp
how wide and long and high and deep is the love of Christ,
and to know this love that surpasses knowledge—that you
may be filled to the measure of all the fullness of God.

EPHESIANS 3:16–19

David and I laughed as we agreed that we felt like two elderly people
who had traded in our gym habits for a leisurely walk up and down our
neighborhood streets. (We were sleep-deprived parents.) I pushed Ocean,
who was more than a year old, in her stroller, while David did his best to
keep four-and-a-half-year-old Ethan on the sidewalk during our evening
family walk with the kids. (The year was 2011, and Everson hadn't been
born yet.) We laughed even harder when we realized we were struggling
to push our children and their vehicles up the hill just a few blocks from
our home, which was in Agoura Hills at the time.

Ocean was giggling, mesmerized by her big brother racing around
with his bike. Ethan kept hopping off his bike to run through neighbors'
yards, eyeing their unique rocks and gathering leaves, until we explained

he couldn't carry them all home. We were rehashing the sweet but typically chaotic day we'd had in the White household.

"Others never see the day-after-day Chinese fire drills of our home life," I said, "or us pole-vaulting over obstacles to rescue each other from some impending parenting catastrophe."

We began listing all the craziness that kids bring into parents' lives, with an emphasis on the outrageous and hilarious chaos of trying to balance marriage, children, finances, household chores, a business, and doctor appointments. Before we knew it, we were doing what we often did—spinning out imagined scenes for some screenplay, this one a comedy about a family where everything that can go wrong does go wrong.

Over the next few months, conversations became snatches of script, and we reached out to one of our script writers. As often happens in the movie business, the script sat on the shelf for two years, until Kevin Downes, David's previous business partner before Pure Flix, asked us if we had a comedy script, since he was doing a few pictures with Sony.

We never dreamed that this idea, after undergoing more changes, would eventually land us at Grauman's Chinese Theatre for the gala premiere of the movie *Mom's Night Out*. And so we've come full circle in this book. Back to the red carpet in chapter 1. Though the idea for that movie was born in 2011, it was incomplete. Unfinished. And by the time of its premiere in March 2014, it bore little resemblance to the ideas we first kicked around on our neighborhood walk. But that is as it should be. Every idea needs to start somewhere, and the pathway it will take between conception and completion is unknown.

A WORK IN PROGRESS

So it is with me. I bear little resemblance to the six-year-old girl who felt small and weak in comparison to my brother and cousins. And I've been transformed since I was the anorexic teenager, the Playboy Mansion guest hanging out by the pool, the naive new believer, and the idealistic new bride. I've been a work in progress by the Maker of the universe since I was conceived, and I remain a work in progress until I'm called into heaven.

And so it is with this book. I began writing during the filming of the sitcom *Hitting the Breaks*, when I truly felt at the end of my rope. Months have passed as I've taken a new look at my story from its beginning until now. There I've gained some new perspectives—eternal perspectives—on what it means to live perfectly unfinished. In the midst of the turmoil over my physical maladies, it seemed I was asking the same old questions I had been asking my whole life and that I had no more answers than I'd had before. All I was seeing at the time, no matter what attempts I made to focus elsewhere, was suffering on top of suffering, loss upon loss, barriers blocking the way to my dreams, trials that led only to new trials, and answers that I didn't have. And all of that left me feeling angry at God, horribly guilty, and disappointed in myself for offering such an imperfect response to the heavenly Father who saved me.

But now as I close this book and this chapter of my life, I see that God is the author, not me. He is the pioneer and perfecter of our journey, and of my faith.

God was whispering to me when I was six years old in my response to Mattie's mother, as I instinctively sensed that families are supposed to be a place of nurture that point to God and his love. God designed me to be drawn to that light and truth, and I was. His fingerprints were on my soul from the beginning.

As I grew through childhood, the labels and messages that told me I didn't matter hurt me—because *I was created to matter*, to be significant to God and this world. God made me for his good pleasure and his purposes, and we are meant to discover and grow into our purpose, not to have it trampled or discouraged.

In looking back at how I cared for my little brother, I see that, despite my home experience, God's image within led me, though only a child myself, to mother him as best I could. God had gifted me with a nurturing spirit, even at that young age, and he built up my confidence that I was created to give to and love others.

In my preadolescent and early teen years, my God-given conscience told me that my mother's actions were wrong, but in brokenness, I took on her shame, and those thoughts held me captive. What a lesson on the power of words and thoughts, so that today, I have learned the importance of taking every thought captive. My past is not a loss, but a gain, for I am who I am today because of the brokenness in my life. God doesn't make mistakes. He didn't give me the wrong circumstances or family, and though we are all less than perfect, they were the perfect parents and family for me, destined by God from the beginning.

By my late teens and early twenties, even though I had become a champion of self-destruction, the strength and determination of a fighter emerged in me—though I was fighting for the wrong things. I was my own worst enemy. Here I see God's miraculous protection, keeping me from death and allowing me to grow—and in so doing, preserving me to become a fighter when the road wasn't easy.

As for the Playboy Mansion, I look back with such compassion at the anchorless girl I was, the one who walked among those rooms of rebellion and brokenness. God allowed me to reach the end of myself, to discover that the promises of that mansion and of those partying days were empty. And once I had groveled there long enough to see that for myself, God dramatically, miraculously intervened in my life and made this promise to me: "In My Father's house are many mansions; if it were not so, I would have told you. I go to prepare a place for you. And if I go and prepare a place for you, I will come again and receive you to Myself; that where I am, there you may be also" (John 14:2–3 NKJV).

God even used such a place as the Playboy Mansion to foreshadow for me that there was a perfect mansion coming. In fact, I recall that in my earliest visits to the mansion, I felt a sense of relief, because no one there would judge me. Now I know of my mansion in heaven where I will never again be judged.

I see now that during my entire life, God has been preparing me for that heavenly home. There, and there alone, will I know fully what it is to be perfect, complete, and lacking in nothing. Every good thing prior to that is but a glimpse of wondrous gifts ahead, and everything negative thing prior to that is but a shadow of all the evil that will be overcome.

The same is true for you. You can revisit the major milestones of your own life and see how God has been at work to mold, shape, and use you as his jar of clay, and then fill you with his treasure. No matter how messy those milestones were. Or shameful. Or heartbreakingly painful. Or powerfully positive.

God was at work in the early years of your life, planting seeds and drawing you toward him.

God was at work in circumstances leading up to your conversion—in ways you never knew. He was there in the most tragic, painfully dark moments when you felt alone and helpless.

God has been at work since your conversion, perfecting and completing you, orchestrating each encounter with the people who cross your path.

God is still at work today, and if you determine to keep your focus on Jesus, to always run toward him and never away from him no matter what, God will transform you in the midst of life's struggles now and in the future.

Even in those times when you feel angry, defeated, or abandoned, God is still at work. Your feelings do not change who God is or what he is doing in you. God uses the darkness to make his light shine brighter. He uses the hardships to strengthen your faith and your character. And for those who love him, God promises that in all things he is working for their good and for his glory (Romans 8:28).

Learning to see our lives today—our present—with eyes wide open to God at work doing something good, no matter how bad the present seems, is a huge challenge. And in the writing of this book, I've discovered how helpful it is to take a new look at the timelines of our lives and make some choices. Will we live in a shortsighted way, or will we be eternity minded?

God's timing is so awesome. Within days of finishing this book, my family gathered at my home to celebrate my dad's sixty-seventh birthday. What a wonderful reminder that the human family, despite all our flaws and imperfections and checkered paths, is a picture of God's family—and he and he alone is the perfect parent. Dad and Carol continue to love each other and all of us, just as they are dearly loved. Jason is flourishing in the field of medical technology and is now a wonderful father himself with a son of his own. We see each other every few months, and although he still picks on me, we adore each other and enjoy giving each other advice. As for Josh, he will forever be my little brother, and we continue to be close as we always have been. He is now thriving as a contractor and is a loving husband to his wife, Korey, and father to their two precious children. My mom is still living in the Midwest. We try to FaceTime monthly and see each other a few times a year. The visits are sweet, and I savor any time when she can be with us. I am so grateful whenever we get to spend time together. To this day I've been trying to convince her to move to California.

I'm often reminded that life on earth is short, and I want to have no regrets. So I continue to create wonderful memories with my family. I treasure them all and am so grateful for the restoration that God has given. As if to prove the point that life is messy and we all are messy, we agree to disagree on many occasions, but we also love to laugh and make fun of each other, knowing that love covers all.

Hebrews 12:1–2 takes on an entirely new meaning for me now: "And let us run with perseverance the race marked out for us, fixing our eyes on Jesus, the pioneer and perfecter of faith." We and we alone choose where we fix our eyes. Making a firm decision to go through life with my eyes focused on Jesus—constantly on the lookout for how he is working in me to make me more like him—is changing everything for me.

Or maybe, keeping myself honest, I should say I am dedicating myself to *learning* to train my eyes on Jesus and to consider myself his work in progress *so that* I can learn to run the race marked out for me—my life—with perseverance. He is going about the work of refining our faith, once shaky and unstable, into absolute perfection—a work that will not be completed until we enter eternity with him. While we are preoccupied with today and next week and next year, God is molding and shaping us to live as eternal beings. Choosing to take the long view of *who we are becoming* means making an intentional choice to keep seeing our lives with an eternal perspective.

I'm not there yet . . . not even close.

Wouldn't you know that even while this book was in production, the remnants of my eating disorder tried to resurface after the nausea from some severe migraines triggered vomiting. This resulted in the return of old patterns. I'd had nine years of complete freedom from binging and purging, but in the past three years, I've fallen a handful of times when the agonizing pain of a debilitating migraine hit. The old horrific feeling of vomiting— something I want nothing to do with anymore—knocked me down in my weakest moments. I hadn't done it to control my weight or feelings as I had in the past, but even so, I felt like such a failure. Self-hatred and condemnation reared their ugly heads once more, and the enemy jumped at the chance to tell me I was a fraud. *You've told your readers you were healed, but that was just your pride speaking,* he whispered. *You aren't healed at all. You are still a failure as a Christian, too weak in your own faith to walk in victory.*

Praise God, I recognized the voice of the enemy and returned to the voice of God instead. *Run with perseverance the race marked out for you, my beloved Andrea. Keep fixing your eyes on Jesus, the pioneer and perfecter of your faith. I have begun a good work in you, and I will bring it to completion.* This is the voice I can trust! My journey from hurting girl to work-in-progress woman continues. When we fall, we must never give up. Whether we're living in victory or recovering from a fall, God loves us no more and no less, because his love is total and unconditional and filled with grace. I pray that every reader grasps this: until we fully receive God's love, we won't fully love ourselves, and so God will get our attention and let us know we still have some work to do!

Still unfinished, I'm moving closer to completion in Christ every step along the way, understanding now that our imperfections are simply those places in our lives that haven't been completed yet. Rather than red flags of self-condemnation, rather than stoplights at dead ends, we can learn to see our unfinished places as spotlights on where God is still at work.

TRADING IN THE VENEER OF PERFECTIONISM FOR THE ARMOR OF GOD

Many of us don't realize that all too often we've turned to perfectionism—our desire to be perfect and in control and our intolerance of our own flaws and weaknesses—when we encounter the pain and suffering of life's battles. Perfectionism is all about performance. It's all about self-sufficiency. It's all about doing enough and doing it flawlessly—looking for ways to find and keep control when our circumstances are out of our control.

But that impossible goal is out of our reach. Instead, God tells us our goal is to run the race that is set before us. That involves forward motion driven by love. Did you know that God's Word doesn't say "win the race"? It doesn't! It says *run* the race. It's that fine line between moving toward Jesus versus moving toward our own good deeds or perfectionism. If we strive to be perfect, even scripturally perfect, we've gone off course again. The Pharisees tried to be perfect at obeying the law instead of deepening a relationship with God, but they failed the important test—recognizing the Son of God and loving God and his people.

Running the race with our eyes fixed on Jesus is not about *doing* (striving for some sort of Christian perfection—exchanging one perfectionism for another); it's about *being* in relationship with Jesus. In relationship with one another. Just as we are. Imperfect, but infinitely loved.

In short, perfectionism tells us a lie. It is merely a cheap veneer that tries to cover over where we fall short, and it does us no favors at all. Let's take off that veneer and replace it with something we really need—something that will serve us well when things are tough.

Trade in *self-confidence* for *God-confidence*.

Trade in the veneer of *perfectionism* for the *armor of God*.

That's what God tells us to do in Ephesians 6:13–18:

> Therefore put on the full armor of God, so that when the day of evil comes, you may be able to stand your ground, and after you have done everything, to stand. Stand firm then, with the belt of truth buckled around your waist, with the breastplate of righteousness in place, and with your feet fitted with the readiness that comes from the gospel of peace. In addition to all this, take up the shield of faith, with which you can extinguish all the flaming arrows of the evil one. Take the helmet of salvation and the sword of the Spirit, which is the word of God.
>
> And pray in the Spirit on all occasions with all kinds of prayers and requests. With this in mind, be alert and always keep on praying for all the Lord's people.

Do you see how God's armor gives us *everything* we need to stand firm?

The belt of truth that surrounds us is the Word of God, so we can fight off the deception of the enemy and our own faulty thinking.

The breastplate of righteousness protects our hearts and is the understanding that we are made right with God only by Jesus' sacrifice for us, not because of anything we can do.

Our feet are ready to run forward in battle to win what? To win *peace*.

And faith in God is our shield that protects us from the enemy's flaming arrows that try to take us out. When his arrows encounter our faith, they will fall powerless to the ground. The enemy cannot penetrate faith!

Salvation is the helmet that protects our brain—the center of our thoughts, our intelligence and understanding, our entire nervous system and life.

Have you noticed that every one of these pieces of armor are passive? They are for protection only. God saves the final piece of armor for last, and it is a proactive piece, our only weapon: God gives us a powerful sword for battle—the Holy Spirit, in whom we are told to pray about everything. *It is God who does battle on our behalf, not we ourselves!* Our job is to remain in him and pray in the power of the Spirit.

I get it now. It really is God who pioneered my faith, and it is God alone who perfects and finishes what he started. God, not me, will finish my faith and complete me. Our job is just to show up as we are and open ourselves wide to all that God wants to accomplish in us and through us.

COME AS YOU ARE

Back in 2010, one Sunday not long after our evening stroll brainstorming idea that would one day become *Mom's Night Out*, we had a chaotic flurry of activity getting the entire family ready for church. I hadn't had time for breakfast, so I grabbed a protein bar as I ran out the door. I hurriedly ate it in the car and stuck the wrapper in my pocket. During the service, I took Ocean back to the nursing room. Another mom, a friend of mine, came in with her three girls—two toddlers and an infant a few months younger than Ocean. She's beautiful—one of those women who always looks perfect on the outside and is truly lovely on the inside as well. And if that isn't enough, she always seems to be wearing brand-name everything, perfectly coordinated.

As we sat side by side nursing and talking, I was hit with the thought, *Oh my, I'm a mess. Why can't I get it together?* She had lost her baby weight already, and I hadn't. When she opened her diaper bag, it was perfectly organized. I'd grabbed my bag on my way out the door with everything from wipes to diapers to teething rings and an extra change of baby clothes tossed in haphazardly. Her hair was perfect, as were as her shoes, dress, jewelry, and purse. All I'd had time for that morning was to grab a top out of the closet to go with a pair of white linen pants (since they go with anything). I'd barely had time to glance in the mirror.

The service ended while we were still in the nursing room. We had just stood up to pack our supplies when my friend said, "Uh, Andrea. You seem to have some, um, brown stuff on the side and back of your pants."

"What?" I craned my neck to see. Sure enough, my chocolate protein bar had left a very noticeable chocolate smudge all over the back and side of my pants. My *white* pants. A chocolate mess ... on my pants. This was not a pretty image. The church we were attending was large, with thousands of people in attendance, meaning I now had to walk past hundreds of people to gather Ethan and find David.

I would have loved to look elegant and all put together like my friend, but that's just not me. (I did try to cover the mess with my diaper bag!) Just about the time I notice that everyone around me is more put together than I am, that's when I'm either tripping on a step or spilling my coffee or breaking a shoe or making some other classy, graceful move. I try to be that feminine, lovely, soft-spoken, elegant, flawless woman, but I'm just the woman with the melted chocolate all over her white linen pants. I'm a mess. That's just me, and I now embrace the fact that the harder I try to hold it all together, the more God shows me that I can laugh at myself, use my klutzy sense of humor, eat a piece of humble pie, and not take myself or my life too seriously. Every. Single. Day.

So I've finally decided that I can celebrate my flaws and can be a mess and not have such high expectations of others. And you know why? Because "though your sins are like scarlet, they shall be as white as snow" (Isaiah 1:18). We are, every single one of us, a mess! God clearly has a sense of humor, and I am gently reminded daily what a mess I am without him. I can't take credit for anything. (I can't even be cool if I try!) We are a never-ending work in progress called to an ongoing daily surrender.

God looks at us, and what does he see? He sees his chosen children. And look what he chose for us: "For he chose us in him before the creation of the world to be holy and blameless in his sight" (Ephesians 1:4).

God himself is the one completing us, perfecting us. That's what he chose us for. And it is God and God alone who makes this promise: "He will also keep you firm to the end, so that you will be blameless on the day of our Lord Jesus Christ" (1 Corinthians 1:8).

So here I stand, a woman who still doesn't get it right, ready to say, "I'm all in, God! Since you say come as you are, then I'm here just as I am. I won't even have to act. It just comes naturally."

I want to show up daily in the world to help make others feel that safe too. I want to be the woman who never judges and who helps others live at peace and celebrate their imperfections. I want to be the one who sits down with friends new and old and says, "My house is a mess; my closet is in shambles; my marriage is a challenge; my body hurts; my plans are confused; I'm flawed; and I'm tired. But I am loved, and so are you! Yes, I am forgiven, and you can be too. I am being perfected and completed not by my own efforts, but by God Almighty in his perfect timing, for his perfect reasons."

I will never be who I want to be or who I think I should be. But when I fall, I will get back up. I will choose to surrender and find joy in the process of God's perfect work in me, because the Perfect One lives inside of me. He is shining though my flaws and weaknesses so that I know it's not I who live, but Christ who lives in me.

I am, for now, perfectly unfinished.

May you continue to discover how to be yourself just as you are. Reflect on your past and look at it, knowing you are redeemed and set free, restored and made new. Know that you are never defined by old labels, broken beliefs, or nagging habits, for no matter what you've been through, he is leading you into his full embrace, beautiful even in your brokenness. Live perfectly unfinished, and never stop seeking him until the day you meet your Creator face-to-face.

ACKNOWLEDGMENTS

First of all, I'd like to thank Shannon Litton, Mike Schatz, and Rachel Pinkerton from 5by5—A Change Agency. Special thanks to Matt Litton, who initially helped me come up with ideas and the title of this book. Thank you for believing in me and making this dream become reality. Y'all make Nashville look really cool. I appreciate the hours of brainstorming and the endless conversations and steadfast encouragement. What a journey it's been, and Lord willing, all will be used for his glory. You all are rock stars!

Cindy Lambert, I am so grateful to work on this project with you. What a gift to have your wisdom, truth, and vision to bring my story to life and help fill it with hope and redemption! Thank you for your friendship, the laughter, the tears, and the hurdles we've endured throughout this process. Oh, how we were constantly reminded of how very perfectly unfinished we are. I love you, sweet friend!

To the incredible team at Zondervan, I can't thank you enough for the months of tedious work and dedication you have given this book. I am forever grateful for the gift you have given me to share with the world what started out as a big dream that has been in my heart for decades. I couldn't be in better hands and am proud and honored to be represented by you all! Special thanks to David Morris, publisher; Sandy Vander Zicht, associate publisher and executive editor; Estee Zandee, editorial assistant; Dirk Buursma, production editor; Brandon Henderson, marketing director;

Curt Diepenhorst, senior art director; Kait Lamphere, senior designer; and Robin Barnett, publicity director.

To Mani and the entire team at Sandoval Design, thank you for your endless hours of help with social media and marketing. You guys are awesome, and I appreciate you all more than words can express!

To Christine McCrudden, my amazing soul sister, who is impeccable at everything you put your hand to. Thank you for your photography and for the talent and creativity behind the scenes. I love you, dear friend. Keep shining!

To David, my amazing husband, who always has my back and is my biggest cheerleader. Your heart and your dedication to the Lord, our beautiful children, and me are incredible. God knew what he was doing when he picked you for me. I am in awe of your patience and perseverance as we've gone through many storms in life. You've remained steadfast, optimistic, prayerful, and surrendered. I am honored to walk by your side year after year. What a gift it has been to go through life with the hardest-working man and super daddy I know. I love you, babe!

To my three undeserved most precious gifts—my children—God has used you in more ways than I can ever explain. You've given me the roles of a lifetime. You are my angels, and above any accolades, being your mama is my greatest achievement on earth. You make my heart sing and the sun shine brighter. The moment I laid eyes on each of you and held you in my arms, my heart became complete. To our baby in heaven, I look forward to meeting you with Jesus, and my heart will never forget when I first heard your heartbeat. I don't understand why I didn't get to meet you here on earth, but you are in the most beautiful place, sweet one.

Ethan, my firstborn, you are my gentle giant, and I am in awe of your love and patience for your little sissies, and oh, what a kindhearted boy you are! God gave you to me when I was in the pit of darkness and used you to pull me through and give me hope again. Your amazing athletic ability and love for sports are infectious. I am so proud of you, my sweet son. Don't ever stop dreaming of being the next white boy in the NBA. I love you, E!

Ocean, my little lady, who loves to dance and sing and wear everything sparkly. You are my little muse. I thank the Lord for giving me eyes to see your sensitive spirit, and he has shown so much of you in me. I am so proud of your effortless grace and talent in ballet and your love for music, singing, and acting. Always remember to dance like nobody's watching, and most of all, dance for an audience of one. I love you, my princess!

Everson, my little Roo Roo, oh, what a little ham you are! You will always be the baby, and you have us wrapped around your finger. You have been through so much already, and your feisty spirit, blonde ringlets, and baby blue eyes keep us on our toes. You are the perfect combination of a princess and a bruiser, and it has been a joy to watch you grow and flourish. I love you, my angel!

Keep shining, my babies, and don't ever forget how much your mama always loves you! Remember to keep Jesus first, and don't ever forget who he made you to be. Life is hard, and I promise he is the answer to every heartache. You can do all things through Christ, who strengthens you. I love you to the moon and back!

To Mom, I want you to know that no matter how old I am, I always want you around, especially in the hard times. I know we didn't have the ideal relationship growing up, but I love you for all you did to support us, and that you never stopped working. I am still in awe that you attended almost all of our sports activities and never complained about the two jobs you had to work. I enjoy my memories as a child looking up to you as my beautiful mama. The best is yet to come, and I love you!

To Dad, my "Pops," I take after your many personality traits. Thank you for always knowing who was good in your book. Your keen discernment has never been off. Thank you for giving this broken, hurt teen the master bedroom when I demanded it after a rough transition. You were beyond generous. Thank you for telling me I was a born actress and belonged on the set of a soap opera. I also appreciate that you passed down the "neat freak" gene. And thank you for your Greek olive skin. I love you, Daddy-O!

To Jason and Josh, for being the most kindhearted and sweetest brothers a sister could ask for. I love you both more than words can express, and I cherish all of our childhood memories—the good, the bad, and the ugly. It is truly a miracle that we survived so many freak accidents while growing up. Even though I was the target, I always knew you'd be there for me in a second if anyone tried to mess with me. Thanks for not letting me go in the house until I threw like a boy. I love you, nerds!

To my grandparents, I love you with all my heart. I hold on to my memories growing up. They are some of the fondest. There's nothing like the comfort of Grandma's and Grandpa's hugs, delicious food, and solid faith. I love you all!

To all my childhood friends and people in past relationships that are unfinished, I am deeply sorry and ask for your forgiveness if we never got to finish where we left off. Please know I am smiling at you and want to give you hugs. You know who you are. Thank you for crossing paths with me. I adore you!

To all the incredible friends who have been there for me through the roller coaster of life, thank you for your beautiful grace and mercy toward me. I love you all for your encouragement.

Finally, none of this would be possible without my Lord and Savior, Jesus Christ. Thank you for continuing to heal this girl who loves and chases you endlessly, wrestles you with her stubbornness, and desires to always "get it right" for you. I pray when I meet you in heaven, you will say, "Well done, good and faithful servant." I pray that you will use my brokenness to beautify, heal, and encourage others. Thank you for your infinite love and mercy.

ANDREA LOGAN WHITE is an actress, a producer, and the co-owner of Pure Flix Entertainment. She and her husband, David A. R. White, enjoy developing and creating films that offer messages of hope and encouragement. Andrea lives in Los Angeles, where she continues to develop scripts, pursue her acting career, and relish her favorite role of being a wife to David and mom to their three children. She has appeared in TV shows, such as *Fear Factor* and *Hitting the Breaks*, and has starred in such films as *Marriage Retreat* and *Moms' Night Out*. Follow @AndreaLoganWhite on Instagram, visit @AndreaLoganWhitePage on Facebook, and connect at AndreaLoganWhite.com.

CINDY LAMBERT is a freelance collaborative writer and editor with more than three decades of book industry experience. She and her husband, Dave, own Somersault (SomersaultGroup.com), an innovative publishing services company that serves authors, agents, publishers, and Christian ministries.